TRANSITIONAL DESIGN
REDEFINING RESIDENTIAL ARCHITECTURE

BASSENIAN | LAGONI ARCHITECTS

Bassenian | Lagoni
ARCHITECTURE • PLANNING • INTERIORS

A Book By Bassenian | Lagoni Architects
Copyright © 2018 by Bassenian | Lagoni Architects

All rights reserved. No part of this publication may be reproduced, stored in a retrieval system or transmitted, in any form or by any means, electronic, mechanical, photocopy, recording or otherwise, without prior written permission from the Publisher. However, brief excerpts may be quoted in a book review.

Library of Congress Control Number:
2017937386

International Standard Book Number:
ISBN 13: 978-0-9721539-9-7 (hardcover)
ISBN 10: 0-9721539-9-3 (hardcover)

Published by Bassenian | Lagoni Architects
2031 Orchard Drive, Suite 100
Newport Beach, CA 92660-0753
Phone: 949-553-9100
Fax: 949-553-0548
www.bassenianlagoni.com

Corporate:
Chairman: Aram Bassenian, AIA
Chief Executive Officer: Carl Lagoni, AIA
President: Jeffrey LaFetra, AIA
Director of Design: David Kosco, AIA

Senior Principals: Scott Adams, AICP
　　　　　　　　　Steven Dewan, NCARB
　　　　　　　　　Ken Niemerski, NCARB

Principals: Hans Anderle
　　　　　　Jeff Ganyo, Architect
　　　　　　Mark Kiner, AIA
　　　　　　Brian Neves, AIA
　　　　　　Cindy Teale, Architect

Book Production
Editorial Director: Aram Bassenian, AIA
Editor-in-Chief: Rickard Bailey, Bailey Consulting
Editor: Heather McCune
Writer: Camilla McLaughlin
Design/Art Director: Edie Motoyama
Art Director/Designer, Cover Design: Zareh Marzbetuny, ZM Design
Floor Plan Graphics: Edie Motoyama, Michael Stone
Assistant to the Editor: Cortney McGerty

Prepress by Toppan Hong Kong

Printed in China by Toppan Printing

10 9 8 7 6 5 4 3 2 1

FOREWORD BY ARAM BASSENIAN, AIA — 7
INTRODUCTION BY JEFFREY T. LAFETRA, AIA — 9
DESIGN TIMELINE BY CARL LAGONI, AIA & DAVID KOSCO, AIA — 11

CONTENTS

01 RETHINKING TRADITIONAL FORMS

| 01 | MODERN FARMHOUSE
RESIDENCE | 14 |
| 02 | CONTEMPORARY TRANSITIONAL
RESIDENCE | 22 |
| | ELEMENTS OF DESIGN
SUSTAINABILITY | 33 |
| 03 | ESCALA
RESIDENCE TWO | 34 |
| 04 | VERMILLION
THE COMMUNITY | 40 |
| 05 | TRILOGY AT VISTANCIA
THE COMMUNITY | 44 |
| 06 | PRAIRIE-INSPIRED CONTEMPORARY
PRIVATE RESIDENCE | 48 |
| 07 | CALIFORNIA COASTAL
PRIVATE RESIDENCE | 52 |
| 08 | LEGACY CLUB AT GREENWOOD
COMMUNITY BUILDING | 54 |

02 TRANSITIONAL ELEMENTS

| 09 | ARTESANA
RESIDENCE ONE | 58 |
| 10 | ARTESANA
RESIDENCE TWO | 66 |
| | ELEMENTS OF DESIGN
MULTI-GENERATIONAL SPACES | 75 |
| 11 | ARTESANA
RESIDENCE THREE | 76 |
| 12 | CASAVIA
THE COMMUNITY | 80 |
| 13 | TREVION
THE COMMUNITY | 84 |
| 14 | WOODSON
THE COMMUNITY | 92 |
| 15 | TRILOGY AT THE POLO CLUB
CLUBHOUSE | 96 |

03 NEW-CENTURY DESIGN

| 16 | AXIS
RESIDENCE FOUR • WALL | 106 |
| 17 | AXIS
RESIDENCE THREE • FRAME | 114 |
| | ELEMENTS OF DESIGN
FORMS + MASSING | 123 |
| 18 | AXIS
RESIDENCE ONE • SKY | 124 |
| 19 | EVERLY
THE COMMUNITY | 132 |
| 20 | MINIMALIST MODERN
PRIVATE RESIDENCE | 136 |
| 21 | 91 SAN VICTOR
MULTI-FAMILY COMMUNITY | 140 |
| | ELEMENTS OF DESIGN
COLORS + MATERIALS | 145 |
| 22 | ALTAIR
CLUBHOUSE | 146 |
| 23 | TOWN SQUARE
MASTER PLAN | 148 |

ANNOTATED PROJECTS LIST — 156
STAFF — 160

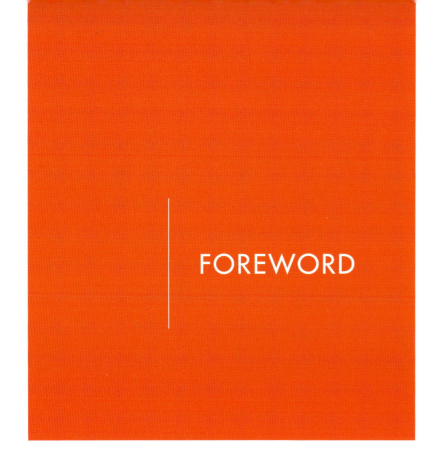

FOREWORD

BY ARAM BASSENIAN, AIA
CHAIRMAN

Toward A Modern Sensibility

There is change in the air .... it is a welcomed movement toward a fresh, clean and simpler vocabulary in residential architecture. We define this change as *"transitional"*—as in a transition from traditional authenticity to modern sensibility.

To be sure, *transitional design* can, at one end of the continuum, be grounded in a familiar aesthetic that adheres to a cultural or geographic precedence. On the other end, it can be completely liberated in its essence and freed from all antecedents, becoming simpler in line and new in detail, embracing a more modern vernacular. Yes, convention can now be dismissed, formulaic habits abandoned, and a new blending introduced to expand our design horizons. This is not a search for a fixed destination. This change is meant to allow exploration toward a more progressive aesthetic. We strongly believe that the resultant impact will be variety in the exterior of our homes and diversity that will beautify our residential streets.

In the homes and buildings featured here you will find designs that lean forward, yet discover that the guiding principles of advanced residential design are not compromised. Inside, the major change is the welcomed disappearance, based on changing lifestyles, of the formal Living Room.

This change gives impetus to more creativity in floor plans. The new-found square footage is reallocated with practical sensitivity throughout the design, giving these homes a larger and more open sensation. Thus, as would be expected, the Great Room takes a consistently more dominant presence.

Outside, a more current look emerges on the elevations with cleaner lines and often more youthful colors. *Transitional Design* embraces the use of new materials and new detailing in fresh compositions. Key elements of the design address a new resolve toward sustainability, respect for the natural environment, human scale, balance, and the use of more comfortable proportions.

The goal of this book is to document a break from the reliance on historicism in design. We are attempting a very conscious step up and a step out. *Transitional Design* is an evolving aesthetic, home grown, and the product of a purely American art form practiced by our own homebuilding industry. So, travel with us, share the joy and excitement in the reinvention. And since the journey has only just begun, view it as a work in progress by a group of highly committed builders and design professionals *in transition* to a new territory.

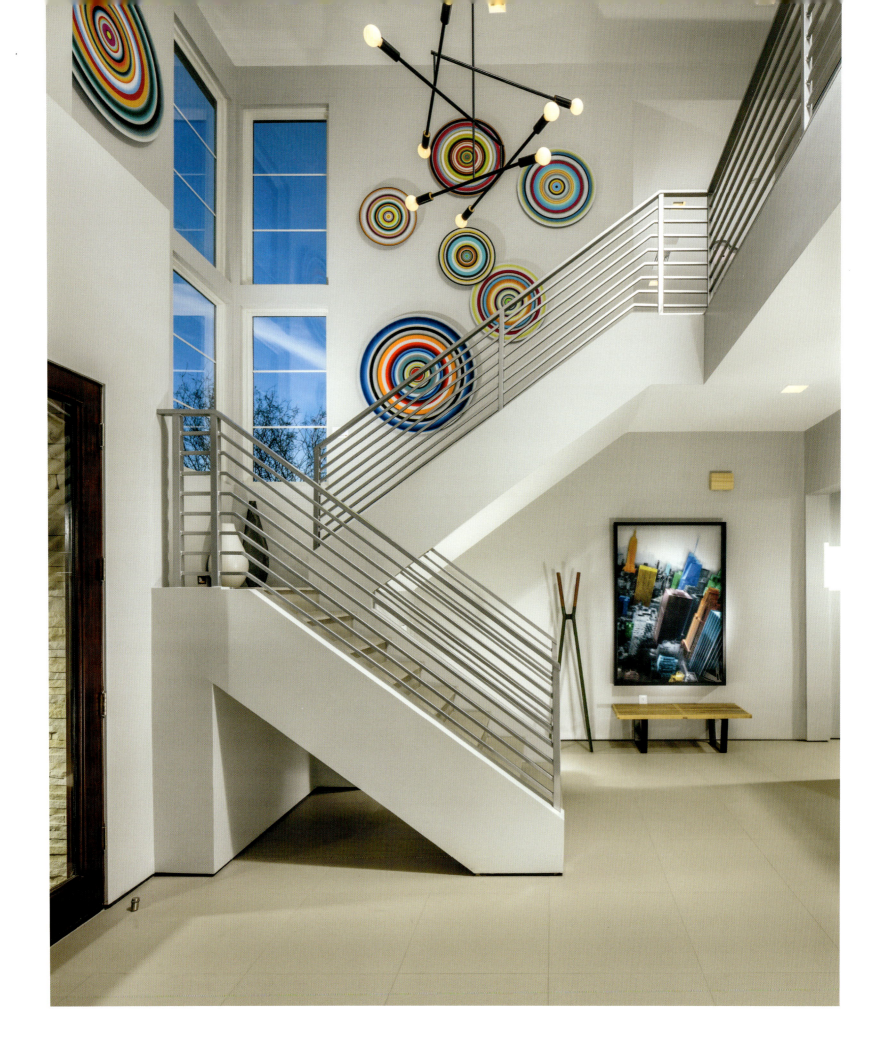

INTRODUCTION

BY JEFFREY T. LAFETRA, AIA
PRESIDENT

"Architecture should speak of its time and place, but yearn for timelessness."

–Frank Gehry

Housing design has always been a dynamic process of innovation and evolution, embracing technological advances in materials and evolving consumer preferences. More than ever, these times are exciting for architects as we create new visions for home. Our design must respond to many different demands as we repurpose land in our urban markets or design suburban neighborhoods for all generations of homebuyers.

The challenge for an architectural firm is to understand the nature of change itself, and to be willing and flexible enough to allow change to occur. As specialists in residential design, we have had the distinct honor to design homes for more than forty years. We take great pride in knowing that our work has the ability to improve the quality of life for people that call our designs "home."

In understanding the fundamental principles of architecture and how to apply them, we help our builder clients bring new homes to market. Great architectural firms are built on exceptional design; however, the commitment to uncompromising service is the foundation on which we build client relationships. We are truly thankful for the opportunity to work with so many clients throughout the United States and around the globe who embrace change and share our passion to be the very best.

None of this would be possible without the family we call Bassenian | Lagoni. We have an office culture that allows for growth and individual expression, while maintaining a commitment to the founding principles of our firm. Without this talented staff, none of these homes would exist.

In the pages of this book we highlight the latest evolution in housing —transitional architecture. We invite you to enjoy and learn from the projects in this, our fourth book. These homes and communities speak to both time and place, while embodying the timelessness that we strive to achieve. We hope you will find inspiration in this book and that it becomes the useful resource it was created to be.

As I reflect on our work, I am reminded of the guiding words of Aristotle: *"We are what we repeatedly do. Excellence, then, is not an act, but a habit."*

DESIGN TIMELINE

BY CARL LAGONI, AIA
CHIEF EXECUTIVE OFFICER

AND

DAVID KOSCO, AIA
DIRECTOR OF DESIGN

A Necessary Evolution

Evolution—the process by which different kinds of living organisms are thought to have developed and diversified from earlier forms during the history of the earth.

The process—the development and diversification of forms—applies to housing in much the same way as it does in nature. Throughout American history, houses have come in a variety of forms: humble structures in small town and farms; opulent mansions of the country's elite; teaming apartments in the fast-growing cities. The range of architectural styles was just as vast—from Colonial to Revival, Queen Anne to Tudor.

This individuality and diversity began to change in the post-World War II era when the demand for housing exploded. Builders tried to meet this need with homes that could be built quickly, efficiently and affordably. As a result, the artistry of home design began to decline. Single-story homes of modest square footage were the predominant housing type for suburbia, with only a few exceptions.

Residential development until the late 1950s continued this model, with few architects involved in new home design. As society shifted in the 1960s, the country began to see a renaissance in design in all areas —cars, consumer goods, and, yes, housing. Communities began to take on a new look. No longer was the house merely shelter with little thought to its image; or conversely, a structure steeped in some vague architectural history. The house became an expression of the times. From Mid-Century Modern ranch homes of the 50s and 60s to Shed Style of the 70s and 80s, neighborhoods exemplified a new and unfamiliar character, memorialized now as an era.

The 1990s brought about resurgence in historical references, with new home communities rooted in identifiable historic styles. Neighborhoods composed in an eclectic array of architectural vernaculars became the vogue. For the next two decades a more pedigreed architecture, authentic to a snapshot in history, dominated most new developments in America.

Today, we are again rethinking the home inside and out. Specific to the face of the house, we're in a transitional era. The movement of the 60s and 70s rejected history, while the 90s referenced only the past. In creating today's designs, we're adding to the architectural vocabulary, embracing architecture rooted in the past but advanced to the present. The result is the warmth of history fused with the sophistication of modern technology and materials. In short, it is architecture that is an expression of today with an eye looking decidedly toward tomorrow.

RETHINKING TRADITIONAL FORMS | 01

MODERN FARMHOUSE
RESIDENCE

CONTEMPORARY TRANSITIONAL
RESIDENCE

ELEMENTS OF DESIGN
SUSTAINABILITY

ESCALA
RESIDENCE TWO

VERMILLION
THE COMMUNITY

TRILOGY AT VISTANCIA
THE COMMUNITY

PRAIRIE-INSPIRED CONTEMPORARY
PRIVATE RESIDENCE

CALIFORNIA COASTAL
PRIVATE RESIDENCE

LEGACY CLUB AT GREENWOOD
COMMUNITY BUILDING

MODERN FARMHOUSE

HENDERSON, NEVADA

01

2,525 SQUARE FEET

PARDEE HOMES,
A MEMBER OF THE TRI POINTE GROUP

BOBBY BERK INTERIORS
CHRIS MAYER PHOTOGRAPHY

Architecture doesn't often find a foundation in consumer attitudes, but this innovative home is grounded in insights gained from extensive research with 24- to 35-year-olds who are actively searching for a home. Authenticity, flexible spaces, a two-car garage, outdoor living and energy efficiency all emerged as must-haves.

What makes this plan a game-changer are options to use rooms in multiple ways, enabling the home to be tailored to an owner's preferences and respond to evolving lifestyles. Also novel is the inclusion of opportunities for additional income to help someone starting out maintain homeownership. Add to that a HERS score of 23 and a roof design that allows for solar panels no matter how the home is orientated, and it is easy to see that this plan establishes a new paradigm for entry-level homes.

Above • Inside, the entry reveals a mix of lofty ceilings, warm woods and views in three directions in a design that lives larger than the square footage. Shaker-style pale grey cabinets in the kitchen add to the overall transitional feeling.

About The Plan • To the left of the entry, a flex/airbnb space with a separate entrance, geared for overnight guests, is an option for generating additional income. A future use could be an office. The second-floor loft is another flex space with the potential of being enclosed for an additional bedroom.

A self-contained multi-generational or rental suite on the second floor to the rear of the house completes this very versatile plan.

LEGEND

1. Entry
2. Covered Outdoor Living
3. Flex/Airbnb Space
4. Dining
5. Covered Outdoor Dining
6. Kitchen
7. Great Room
8. Laundry
9. Powder Room
10. Garage
11. Outdoor Dining
12. Outdoor Flex Space
13. Master Bedroom
14. Master Bath
15. Master Deck
16. Bedroom 2
17. Bath 2
18. Loft/Bedroom 3
19. Guest/Multi-Gen/Rental Suite

2,525 SQUARE FEET

Above • A straight stairway and metal balustrades visually integrate the main and second levels and make the home feel more spacious. Wainscoting on the stairway adds a familiar traditional element to soften the otherwise contemporary aesthetic.

Throwing Convention Out the Window

Outdoor living is fundamental to the way this home functions. Glass walls slide or telescope out of sight, and main living areas spill out onto courtyards, decks and covered patios on multiple sides. Even the corner between the great room and dining area vanishes to create one huge outdoor area.

Above • By orienting an entry courtyard toward the interior, architects created a covered outdoor room, which adds another dimension and more square footage to the central courtyard and the main living area.

A second covered area and patio on the opposite side extend the dining area even further. No change in elevation and the same flooring achieves a seamless integration.

Top • Cozy yet expansive are dual options for the great room. A beamed ceiling defines and visually lowers the space, while disappearing glass walls open the entire room to the adjacent courtyard.

Center • Outdoor theater? No problem, with this versatile deck on the opposite side of the great room. Seat backs that disappear into the surface ready it for multiple uses.

Bottom • The master suite is a haven. An adjacent deck becomes a private venue for watching the stars or flickering flames.

Below • A completely separate 384-square-foot flat over the garage with its own entrance is adaptable as a long-term rental to provide a stream of income or as a home office. The living area, top, includes ample room for seating and a streamlined kitchen. A separate bedroom, bottom, makes this space an equally comfortable hideaway for guests.

Pictured Left • It is easy to see how the deck integrates with the interior of the house and adjacent great room. A nearby hammock over a small lawn adds another dimension to this diverse space.

CONTEMPORARY TRANSITIONAL

HENDERSON, NEVADA

02

3,190 SQUARE FEET

PARDEE HOMES, A MEMBER OF THE TRI POINTE GROUP

BOBBY BERK INTERIORS
CHRIS MAYER PHOTOGRAPHY

Designed for the same cohort as the Modern Farmhouse but ten years later, the Contemporary Transitional incorporates elements certain to woo move-up buyers — a connection to the natural environment, lots of venues for entertaining and plenty of storage. Outdoor living is even more central to the experience and function of the home with a well-orchestrated complement of patios, decks and play areas migrating from almost every room. Views of the outside, sun and sky expand interior panoramas. Aspirational features include a dramatic waterfall, an artful pool that becomes a design element and an entire wing devoted to a master suite. A home automation system is another must-have for tech-savvy buyers.

The exterior makes an impressive statement with a mix of modern and contemporary aesthetics. Thick stucco walls and stone cladding, created just for the house, are balanced by a composite material that mimics rusted Corten steel. A central stone tower and graceful arch lend a classic sensibility. Deep overhangs on south-facing sides shade the home in warm months. With a 12 HERS score and a 9.8 kw photovoltaic system, this home achieves a Net Zero status.

About The Plan • An overview illustrates how meticulously outdoor living is integrated into the design. Rooms on three sides of the main level merge with exterior spaces.

The second floor incorporates several decks. A spacious casita behind the garage includes a covered private patio, small kitchen and full bath, opening the door to diverse uses from a guest space to office to fitness room.

LEGEND

1. Entry
2. Dining
3. Kitchen
4. Laundry/Pantry/Home Management
5. Great Room
6. Outdoor Living
7. Outdoor Dining/Kitchen
8. Flex/Multi-Gen Suite
9. Powder Room
10. Garage
11. Outdoor Family Room
12. Bedroom 2
13. Bath 2
14. Bedroom 3
15. Teen Loft
16. Master Bedroom
17. Master Bath
18. Private Home Office
19. Master Deck

3,190 SQUARE FEET

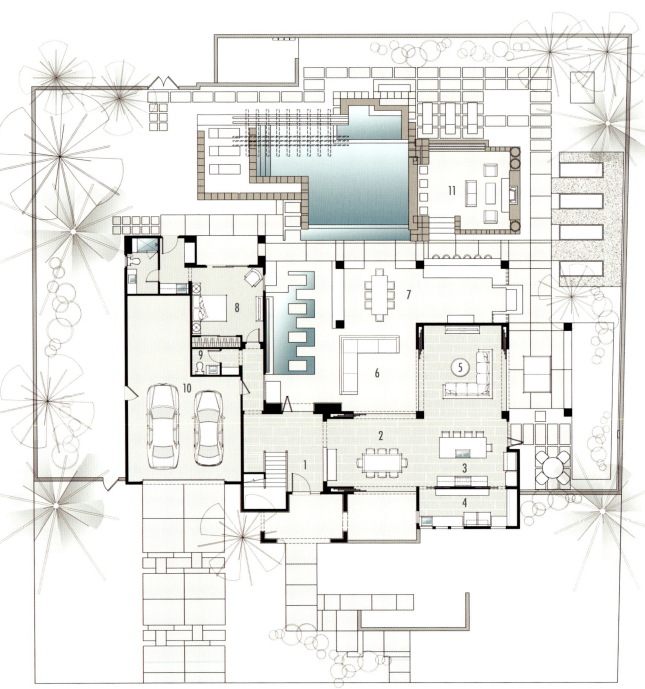

Top • Central to the landscape is a covered outdoor kitchen and bar flanked by spacious alfresco dining. The outdoor kitchen's blue tile and cabinetry echo the color used in the main kitchen.

Center • An open-air great room—set outside in the sunken patio—is an intimate space, ideal for entertaining. Ample seating, fireplace and television amp up the appeal as a place to kick back.

Bottom • A large central kitchen island is an essential, whether it's a setting to showcase food or simply kibitz with the cook. A work area sheltered behind the blue wall is a forward-looking design concept offering space for storage, food prep, even crafts.

Left • A floating staircase flanked by windows makes a dramatic statement in the entry.

Above • The dining area merges an outdoor living room on one side and an entry courtyard oriented to the interior on the other.

Below • Water views that at once calm and energize ripple throughout the home. The patter of water falling from the green wall injects a soothing element, while patches of greenery guide the eye toward the pool and distant gardens. Open and covered spaces weave together seamlessly as dramatic lighting showcases the evening landscape.

Right • Sightlines from the foyer lead all the way to back and side yards, establishing an essential connection with nature. Disappearing glass walls promote an easy flow between all the main entertaining areas. The vibrant red of the back wall of the great room is a focal point anchoring the entire main floor and even becomes an important ingredient in the exterior elevation.

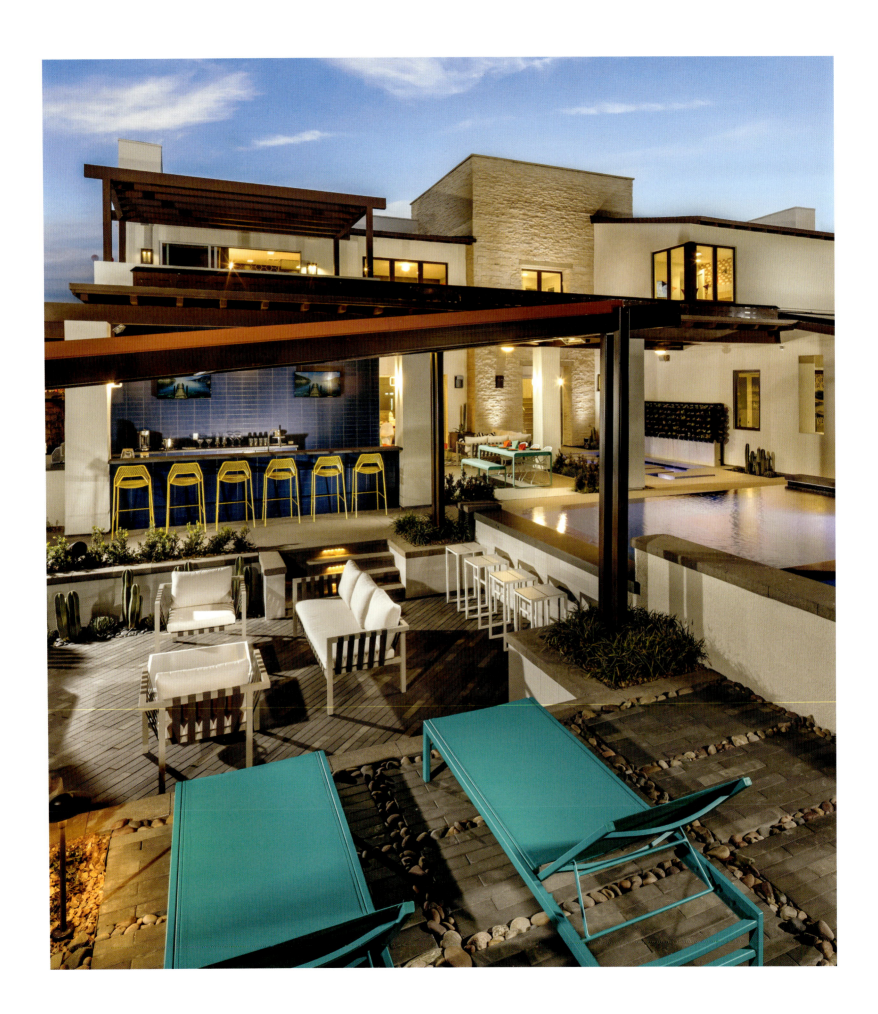

Left • The view from the back of the property shows how roof lines complement each other and how well the overlay of outdoor spaces has been executed.

Above • An extensive master suite includes a spa bath and separate office.

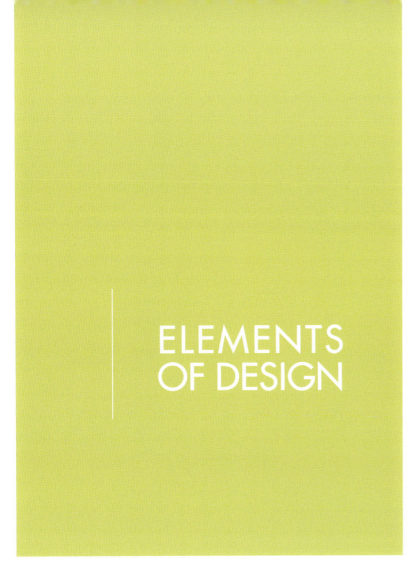

ELEMENTS OF DESIGN

SUSTAINABILITY

The outpouring of new products and the number of certifications might make sustainable appear complicated, but, in essence, it distills down to using the fewest amount of natural resources for the least impact on the environment. No longer amenities, sustainability and energy efficiency are integral to transitional architecture, beginning with how space is organized. Optimal plans group the internal mass of the house to use electricity, water, heating, lighting and cooling most economically. Typically, this means combining spaces that will be occupied at the same time. Another structural component—thick walls—accommodates additional insulation for heating and cooling.

A strong indoor-outdoor connection addresses sustainability as well as lifestyle. Opening interiors promotes airflow, reduces reliance on conditioned air and enhances indoor air quality. Creating a progression of outdoor spaces, from covered to open, allows interiors to stay cooler and introduces controlled natural light in the interior. Transitional architecture addresses windows that will receive the most solar exposure with features that fulfill the same role as a traditional awning. However, instead of a solid covering, they might appear as an artful array of metal slats, screening or some other embellishment—but their function is to direct unfiltered solar rays away from interiors.

Managing solar heat gain isn't just a function of filtering light. Rather, at the outset, architects consider the orientation of a home on a lot to create a house designed to be energy efficient. For example, homes designed with a south-facing front incorporate more shade-creating elements into the elevation. Similarly, north-facing homes receive substantially less direct daytime sun and thereby allow for elevations with less movement and cleaner lines.

Many jurisdictions now require solar energy on new homes, but architects look for alternatives to traditional placement of panels. Roofs can be designed to be adapted to a range of building sites and solar orientations. For example, rooflines on the Modern Farmhouse, pictured in the top right photo on the facing page, demonstrate the integration of solar in the overall architecture. Here solar panels provide shade for second-floor windows.

Looking ahead, architects expect to see technology incorporated into structures to make more homes more sustainable. As architecture and building products continue to evolve hand in hand, the overall thermal performance of homes will continue to improve. The day is coming when every home will be able to produce enough—and more—energy to power day-to-day life. Then, the only challenge will be designing homes and neighborhoods that incorporate the technology to store excess energy.

O3

RESIDENCE TWO • 3,063 SQUARE FEET

PARDEE HOMES, A MEMBER OF THE TRI POINTE GROUP

BOBBY BERK INTERIORS
CHRIS MAYER PHOTOGRAPHY

ESCALA

HENDERSON, NEVADA

Timeless and contemporary coexist in this inspired up-to-date vision of Mid-Century Modern. The look, beauty and power of the simple lines celebrated by this vernacular are evidenced in the synergy of shapes that comprise the exterior elevation. Here, a low-pitched sloping roof intersects a central rectangular block made of smooth decorative stone that emulates concrete. Blue batten board and windows that echo the rigorous geometric lines of the roof highlight a third plane. The end result is a fresh, dynamic interpretation of an architectural classic. The entry, pictured right, makes a strong opening statement, while streamlined elements, such as a ceiling enriched with natural wood, preview what lies ahead. The muse might be Mid-Century Modern, but the lifestyle and aesthetic are very much "today."

Below • A spacious lounge area is a centerpiece of the interior. The rich wood and elevation change of the sloping ceiling delineate the space, while focal points such as the bold geometric pattern surrounding the fireplace and the display wall in the media room anchor and make each grouping distinct. Large windows repeat the geometric forms, establishing a connection to the surrounding landscape and infusing the interior with natural light.

Above Right • The linear dance continues with the cabinetry and island in the kitchen. Telescoping walls open the space to a covered patio for outdoor dining.

Below Right • A natural wood ceiling softens the contemporary feeling in the master suite and brings a sense of continuity to the space. A large glass wall makes adjacent patios part of the experience.

Left • This house is anything but mundane. Upscale additions include a dramatic lighted wine room, top, and a spa-like master bath, bottom. Especially striking is the contrast of the sculptural soaking tub with the streamlined finishes in the master bath.

Above • At first glance this home might appear straightforward, but the rear elevation shows that the overall design, even for outdoor spaces, is anything but simple. Beginning with patios and covered lanais near the house, the landscape progresses to a pool, lounge area, seating under a pergola and fireplace. At the center is a covered dining area off the kitchen. A disappearing window opens the adjacent bar to the media room. Splashes of yellow and orange and a whimsical duck enliven the otherwise neutral palette.

VERMILLION

PALM SPRINGS, CALIFORNIA

Mid-Century Modern is Palm Springs' iconic architectural style and interpreting this vernacular without sacrificing authenticity requires finesse. Vermillion honors the principles of the movement in plans that resonate with 21st-century consumers. Here, sightlines expand across interiors and linear forms predominate. An indoor/outdoor synergy organizes almost every space. Transom windows and sloping volume are consistent, but new materials and technologies enable interiors to engage in ways designers never imagined 60 years ago. A variety of roof configurations — peaked, sloping, even butterfly — energize the streetscape, pictured above, and pose a striking, yet harmonic, contrast with the undulating ridges of the mountains in the background.

04

THE COMMUNITY

BEAZER HOMES

INTERIORS BY TRIOMPHE DESIGN
A.G. PHOTOGRAPHY

Top • This versatile respite space is an ideal office, media room or place to share a special vintage with friends. Wood and stone, used in applications impossible a few years ago, add depth and richness, making this room anything but mundane.

Center • Telescoping doors create an 18-foot opening that merges the great room with a covered patio, pool and lounge area. Transom windows—the 21st-century version is pictured here—remain a Mid-Century Modern hallmark. Tile that mimics wood on the fireplace surround is another innovative use of a new material.

Bottom • This well-orchestrated kitchen is dynamic without being overly busy. Transom windows float above the cabinets on the back wall and inject natural light into the room. The island functions as a neutral bridge between the kitchen and dining areas.

Top • Large double-height windows that wrap around a corner emphasize linear forms and also open the master bedroom to views of the mountains. The sloped ceiling, a Mid-Century Modern signature, adds volume, while the warm wood finish cozies up the space.

Center • Details, such as trim highlighted in white and windows that echo the roof lines, take the typical Mid-Century Modern elevation to the next level without compromising the principles of the vernacular.

Bottom • Every opportunity was taken to make a strong statement, and the rear elevation is no exception. A progression of outdoor spaces moves the eye toward the great room.

LEGEND

1. Entry
2. Kitchen
3. Dining
4. Great Room
5. Garage
6. Powder Room
7. Laundry
8. California Room
9. Master Bedroom
10. Master Bath
11. Bedroom 2
12. Bath 2
13. Den/Home Office/Bedroom 3

1,972 SQUARE FEET
RESIDENCE ONE

About The Plan • This plan addresses the limitations of a narrow lot with outdoor connections from almost every room. The great room opens to a covered California Room and progresses to a patio and dining area poolside. Corner and clerestory windows collect natural light and enable the plan to live larger than the square footage. Grouping bedrooms at opposite ends of the house ensures privacy for guests and owners. A third room offers the potential for den, home office or bedroom.

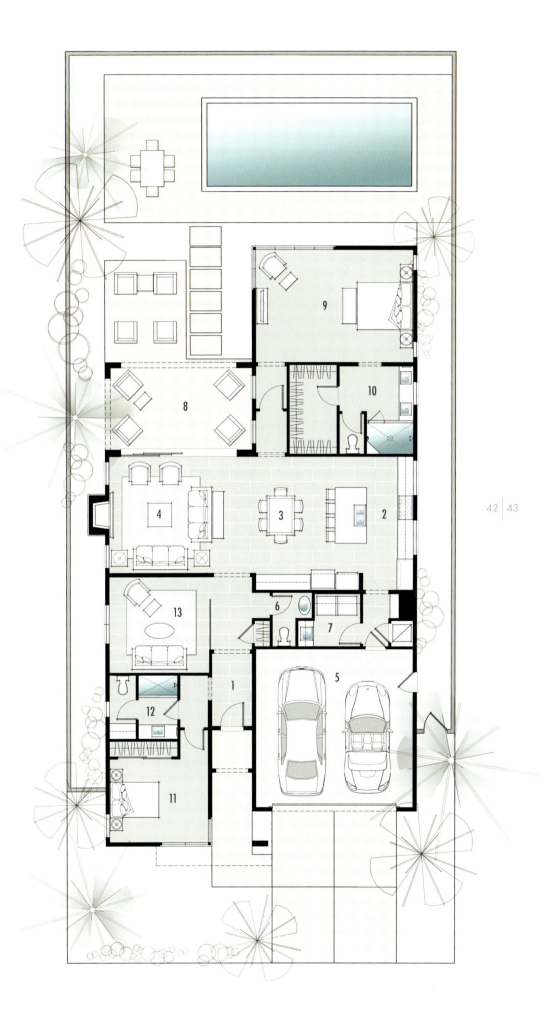

TRILOGY AT VISTANCIA

PEORIA, ARIZONA

05
THE COMMUNITY

TRILOGY BY SHEA HOMES

DESIGN LINES, INC.
MARK BOISCLAIR PHOTOGRAPHY

Architecture responds to the landscape in this new southwest active-adult community. Here, exterior hues interact with a desert palette and roof lines echo the gentle slopes of the mountains that frame the area. A contrasting block feature that wraps around the front corner and window offers a contemporary take on traditional pueblo construction and builds on the progressive expression of the southwestern form. An enclosed courtyard and covered entry are good indications that an indoor-outdoor synergy, essential to both the climate and the lifestyle, is integral to the design.

Top • Entertaining is part of the DNA of these homes. An array of living spaces, including a great room and fireside sitting area, are arranged toward the back of this space, while the kitchen and island take center stage as a hub that ties all the living areas together.

Center • A twelve-foot coffered ceiling adds volume, literally elevating the space, while rustic beams inject an element of warmth. Another dynamic feature–transom glass–lines the walls just below the ceiling and infuses the room with even more light.

Bottom • Extensive outdoor living areas include poolside dining, covered seating and an outdoor living room to the side of the pool. Waterfalls and dramatic lighting transform the pool into an artful addition to the landscape.

Below • Circular shapes in the seating area grouped around a fire pit and an adjacent raised patio form a counterpoint to the linear nature of this design. Tucked into the corner of the covered patio is an outdoor kitchen. Under the eaves, an exposed manufactured beam calls attention to the structure of the building and reflects a progression toward a contemporary aesthetic.

Top Left • A coffered ceiling elevates this plan, emphasizing the rectilinear forms that compose the room. Here, kitchen and great room trade places, with space for the kitchen and dining at the end of the room.

Bottom Left • Large windows open the dining area to the side yard, and the adjacent door leads to a smart space which includes the laundry as well as a flex space for crafts or home management. The use of transom windows remains a significant element.

PRAIRIE-INSPIRED CONTEMPORARY

LOS GATOS, CALIFORNIA

06

PRIVATE RESIDENCE • 5,832 SQUARE FEET

DAVIDON HOMES

CHRIS MAYER PHOTOGRAPHY

A uniquely American vernacular, Prairie style receives an upscale polish in this decidedly modern home. Here, an overlay of horizontal planes and forms, cascading stairs and large overhangs builds organically to create a compelling statement and propel the structure along a saddle-shaped lot.

A liberal use of stone on the elevation and along the foundation anchors the building to the earth, merging it with the surrounding landscape. A stone wall echoes the shape of the exterior and further nestles the home into the hillside. Along with the steep incline and shallow lot, stringent development guidelines and adjacent buildings offered a unique challenge. The home was sited to maximize extensive views of the valley and the city.

The addition of a round turret creates an even more imposing presence. Windows and doors in varied configurations lend a geometric element, making the views part of the interior experience. Numerous terraces and decks, covered and uncovered, flank main living areas as well as the master bedroom and bath

Top • Stone, soft wood tones and an emphasis on geometric shapes, hallmarks of Prairie style, introduce the vernacular into the interior. Mullions on windows and doors were retained but given a contemporary spin.

Left • It's rare to see so much synchronicity between a landscape and a structure. Plant materials and the encircling stone wall echo the neutral color palette and geometric rigor of the exterior.

Bottom • Dramatic paneled ceiling treatments elevate main rooms, including the master suite. French doors and large windows make surrounding greenery a natural backdrop.

07 | CALIFORNIA COASTAL

PRIVATE RESIDENCE • 2,272 SQ. FT.

CAYUCOS, CALIFORNIA

CHRIS MAYER PHOTOGRAPHY

Savvy design begins with the interplay of materials from the siding and copper gutters to the tans, golds and greys of the hardscape in this California coastal home. Making best use of a long narrow corner lot within sight of the ocean was a design objective, as was ensuring the best views inside and out. Innovative features include a glass bridge linking guest quarters over the garage to three bedrooms on the second floor. Large windows and doors open the dining room and office to side and rear patios. A large stone fireplace becomes a focal point for a rear courtyard, while a glass-enclosed deck opens the second floor to the views. An expansive island takes center stage in the kitchen and directs attention through the house to the outdoor fireplace. A disappearing stackable door merges the kitchen and the al fresco dining area in the side yard.

Detail Driven • Offering privacy and views, the front of the home parallels the configuration of the lot and creates an interesting angle for the entry. A second floor deck opens the master suite to sights and sounds of the ocean, while large windows ensure views on the main level. The garden gate provides an entrée to secluded outdoor terraces and a courtyard. The use of copper for gutters and downspouts turns a utilitarian feature into an artful element, almost jewelry for the home.

LEGACY CLUB AT GREENWOOD

TUSTIN, CALIFORNIA

08

COMMUNITY BUILDING • 4,331 SQUARE FEET

STANDARD PACIFIC HOMES

VER DESIGN
A.G. PHOTOGRAPHY

A gathering space for residents of multiple single-family developments, this clubhouse honors the legacy of the setting with a forward-looking vision of transitional architecture. The location is the storied former Tustin airbase whose hangers remain the largest wooden structures ever built. Additionally, the region has a rich agricultural history and these two points of origin served as design inspiration.

The purpose of the building as a main gathering space, communal lounge and kitchen aligns with current development trends, but the form of the structure is reminiscent of traditional farm buildings. Dual rows of clerestory windows with a curved metal roof on the upper level make best use of the tall volume and infuse the interior with light. Linear forms—a contemporary hallmark—are given a refined, up-to-date treatment in the windows. Similar shapes are repeated throughout the interior with a long rectangular disappearing glass wall.

Exterior spaces are so deftly integrated into this design that little or no transitions are required. The patio appears as a logical progression of the gathering places inside. An additional covered side patio is designed for children.

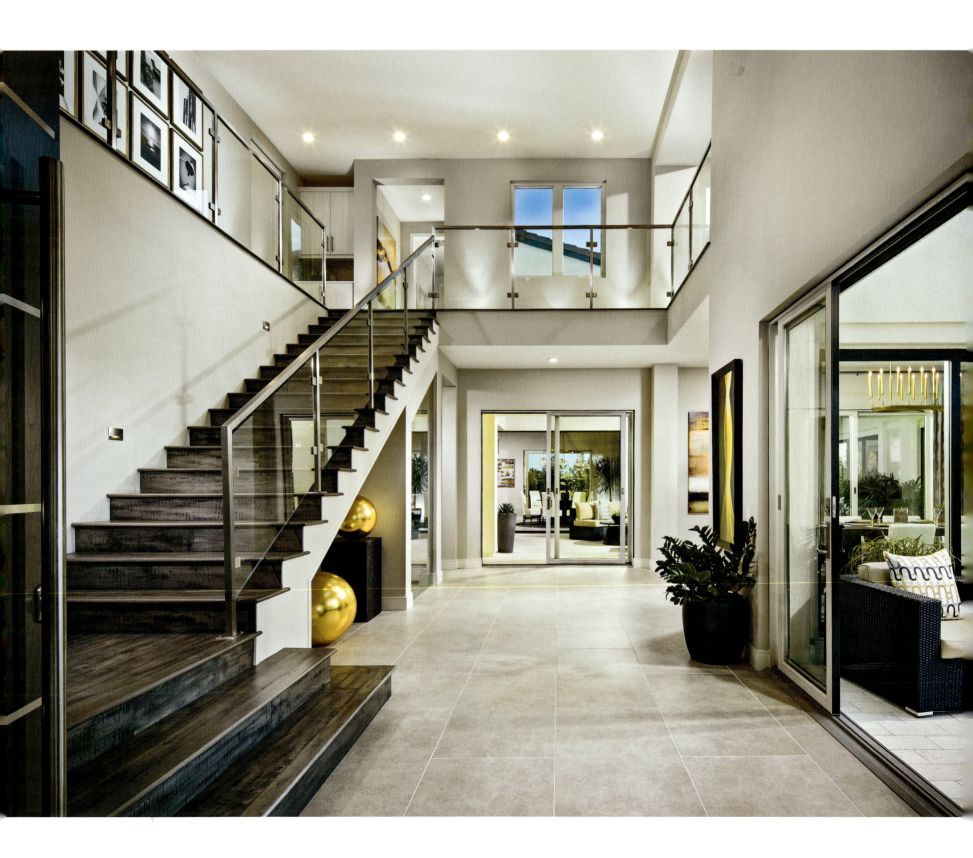

TRANSITIONAL ELEMENTS | 02

ARTESANA
RESIDENCE ONE

ARTESANA
RESIDENCE TWO

ELEMENTS OF DESIGN
MULTI-GENERATIONAL SPACES

ARTESANA
RESIDENCE THREE

CASAVIA
THE COMMUNITY

TREVION
THE COMMUNITY

WOODSON
THE COMMUNITY

TRILOGY AT THE POLO CLUB
CLUBHOUSE

ARTESANA

SAN DIEGO, CALIFORNIA

RESIDENCE ONE • 4,052 SQUARE FEET

PARDEE HOMES, A MEMBER OF THE TRI POINTE GROUP

AMI SAMUEL INTERIORS
ERIC FIGGE PHOTOGRAPHY

Sometimes the most forward-looking designs begin with a look back. When brainstorming residences for a new luxury neighborhood in a gated enclave in Southern California, architects found inspiration in the legacy of Lilian Rice, whose work has become a touchstone for a style synonymous with Rancho Santa Fe.

A lifestyle comparable to a resort and a connection to the landscape also informed their vision. Three unique residences are the result. Each is rooted in an authentic regional aesthetic and designed to respond to evolving lifestyles with a casual elegance that whispers luxury.

Left • From the perspective of the great room, the repetition of the arched form becomes a dynamic element in contrast to the neutral hues and linear composition of the interior spaces.

Above • Each arch is a portal to a different experience. The initial entry arch leads to a beamed loggia where windows open to an adjacent guest casita. The next arch transitions to a central courtyard open to the sky. A third leads to the double wood doors of the main entry.

Right • The master suite and a spacious bath contribute to the overall resort sensibility. Even the master bath visually connects to the outdoors through sightlines. A window over the tub calls for daydreaming and stargazing.

Above • Colors, textures and forms found in nature interplay here creating a calming but energetic vibe. Windows located high on the wall bring in additional light and play up the volume and proportions. A lower ceiling makes the kitchen a distinct space, and, along with wood cabinets, injects a feeling of coziness and warmth.

Left • A composition of strong vertical elements literally elevates the great room. Large rectangular openings to a second-level book loft add drama and offer a visual connection to the room below.

Above • Indoor-outdoor relationships extend to secondary spaces such as this second-floor guest suite. A full complement of patios and outdoor areas brings additional outdoor living possibilities to the rear of the house.

ARTESANA

SAN DIEGO, CALIFORNIA

10

RESIDENCE TWO • 4,726 SQUARE FEET

PARDEE HOMES, A MEMBER OF THE TRI POINTE GROUP

AMI SAMUEL INTERIORS
ERIC FIGGE PHOTOGRAPHY

The imprint of Lilian Rice's Southern California aesthetic is very evident in this imposing home. The interpretation is modern, and the overall plan is individual and unique. The scale is impressive, but intimate spaces provide a balance to the open-concept interior. A sense of elegance further refines the plan, inside and out.

Overall, the architecture is horizontal in its expression. Spanish influences that are a Rice signature are very much on display in the elevation pictured at right. The bank of windows with louvered shutter detail is a modern interpretation of the screened porches found in her designs. A single classic arch delineates the entry. Wood detailing throughout this level, as well as the awnings over the deck and balcony, are traditional Spanish elements, but articulated here with clean, simple lines. In this home, the roof also plays into the overall scheme as a design element.

Left • The delicate lines of this bedroom balcony emphasize the overall mass of the structure. The stucco is simple and modern, but still offers an historical reference to many of the homes Rice designed.

Above • The great room illustrates ways in which larger entertaining spaces transition to smaller, more private areas. An alcove tucked behind the fireplace wall and two-sided hearth is a quiet place for cocktails or conversation. A wall of glass and disappearing doors make the vibrant landscape part of the experience.

LEGEND

1. Entry
2. Entry Porch
3. Entry Courtyard
4. Entry Gallery
5. Interior Entry
6. Great Room
7. Library
8. Kitchen
9. Walk-in Pantry
10. Dining
11. Outdoor Covered Dining
12. California Room
13. Wine Room
14. Casita/Gen-Smart Suite
15. Casita Retreat
16. Powder Room
17. Drop Zone
18. Garage
19. Master Bedroom
20. Master Bathroom
21. Home Office
22. Home Office Deck
23. Loft Study
24. Bedroom 2
25. Bath 2
26. Laundry/Craft Space
27. Bedroom 3
28. Bath 3
29. Cabana
30. Outdoor Kitchen

4,726 SQUARE FEET

About The Plan • A logical progression from public to private areas is central to this design, as are elegance and flexibility. An entry courtyard transitions to interior private areas. Optional spaces include a guest casita, gen-smart suite and wine storage. Courtyards, patios and decks layer both levels with outdoor living opportunities. Functionality is also integral, as manifest in the large laundry room/craft space, and drop zone adjacent to the garage entry.

ELEMENTS OF DESIGN

MULTI-GENERATIONAL SPACES

One of the biggest changes in housing is the growing diversity of buyers, both demographically and culturally. Increasingly, builders and potential homeowners look for homes that can accommodate these differences, especially the vision of home as a place for multiple generations and extended family. Today, the phrase, "extended family," is apt to encompass elderly parents, adult children, siblings or even other adults.

Traditionally, multi-generational spaces implied a casita or a flat over a detached garage, but smaller lot sizes and changes in attitudes regarding family are moving them closer to, or into, the main house. Market demand determines this location and also shapes expectations regarding design, fit and finish. Rather than just a nice bedroom, a multi-gen suite requires a living area spacious enough to be desirable for long-term occupancy. In addition to a private sleeping section, generational suites, such as those pictured left, include a bath that is a little smaller than a master bath but larger than a secondary bathroom, as well as comfortable lounges and a kitchenette outfitted with the basics — a refrigerator, sink and microwave. A separate cooktop is not a necessity, and usually local regulations and permitting determine whether or not one can be incorporated. A stackable washer and dryer is a desirable addition that further positions the suite as a defined living area, rather than simply a place to sleep. Another plus, but not a must-have, is an exterior entry, and some plans even integrate garage space.

The suite, pictured above left, is designed to live larger than the square footage would imply. Extensive windows and sliding-glass doors bring in views and natural light. A connection with the home's outdoor living amenities further energizes the interior and reinforces ties to the main house. The suite also includes a place to dine, as well as several distinct seating areas.

Local market preferences also play into where a generational suite is located, but what is essential, both psychologically and emotionally according to experts, is a connection to the main house. The multi-gen suite, pictured lower left, is located above the garage of the Contemporary Farmhouse and is directly adjacent to a main deck of the home, which includes an outdoor screen and a firepit. With a separate outdoor entry, it offers privacy, while still being fully integrated into the plan. The bedroom occupies a distinct space, apart from the seating area, and the kitchen has all the essentials, including under-counter seating.

Expect generational suites to become an even more desired feature in new homes as the concept of family and home continues to expand and evolve.

ARTESANA

SAN DIEGO, CALIFORNIA

11

RESIDENCE THREE • 5,065 SQUARE FEET

PARDEE HOMES,
A MEMBER OF THE TRI POINTE GROUP

AMI SAMUEL INTERIORS
ERIC FIGGE PHOTOGRAPHY

In the expansive home pictured above, the elevation is a composition of rectilinear forms anchored by a strong vertical element in the center. Stucco mass, wood trim and tile roofs — all Rice keynotes — remain, but the execution is entirely modern with streamlined details such as the railings on the second level. The entry doors offer an additional contemporary expression of these horizontal forms. The tall vertical wall adjacent to the entry runs through the home and functions as an organizational spine for the structure. Many rooms are sequential experiences that progress as one walks through the house. Interior courtyards weave outdoor living into the fabric of the home. The vision of a resort lifestyle is clearly evident. Stacking doors, shown top right, completely open the master suite and bath to a large balcony, making the greens and blues of nature part of the experience. The glass cube and stone backdrop, pictured bottom, transform the shower into an artful element.

Right • The main doors open to an impressive, glass-railed staircase overlooking a long gallery below, a front courtyard on the right and, further down, the entrance to the dining room. Far-reaching sightlines extend past the rear courtyard and great room to outdoor living areas in the backyard.

Above • A second-floor gathering space, shown top, opens to an intimate balcony and outdoor fireplace. Views from the kitchen extend across the great room to one of several outdoor living rooms in the home. The casual dining nook on the right is adaptable to a range of uses.

12 | CASAVIA

THE COMMUNITY | SAN DIEGO, CALIFORNIA

PARDEE HOMES, A MEMBER OF THE TRI POINTE GROUP

STUDIO V INTERIOR DESIGN
CHRIS MAYER PHOTOGRAPHY

San Diego was ground zero for the explosion of Spanish architecture in the early 20th century. Casavia pays homage to this tradition, along with architect Irving Gill and other proponents, but it also reinterprets the style in a fresh, new and appropriate way for the setting. Generous use of wood in horizontal slats, posts, beams and infill between the windows on the exterior, pictured far right, combined with a sculpted stucco mass, creates a composition for transitional architecture with a strong Spanish flavor. Windows are grouped around a corner in a contemporary pattern that also allows for natural light to infuse the interior of the narrow and deep structure. A second-floor balcony and the entry courtyard echo the integration of outdoor living, which is central to both the aesthetic and lifestyle of Southern California.

Opposite Page • Main living areas wrap around a central courtyard, pictured top left. Neutral framing and windows that extend around a corner, top right, lend a sense of airy spaciousness to a small den adjacent to the great room. The kitchen in the model, bottom left, reflects a more transitional feeling. The view from the courtyard, bottom right, shows how living spaces fan out from the kitchen, which is also oriented outside.

Below • In this design, the dining room is situated next to the kitchen at the end of the space. Extensive glass doors open to covered patios on both sides and to an outdoor kitchen.

Right • A traditional, yet powerful, architectural form—a simple arch—heightens the Spanish influence on both elevations, while dark trim surrounding the windows and under the eaves adds to the aesthetic. On the lower elevation, the parabolic arch is expanded to create a dynamic entry.

TREVION
PLAYA VISTA, CALIFORNIA

13

THE COMMUNITY

BROOKFIELD RESIDENTIAL

YOLANDA LANDRUM INTERIOR DESIGN
ARON PHOTOGRAPHY

The next progression in Southern California residential architecture, Trevion pays tribute to a rich heritage while also offering a decidedly contemporary vibe. Detailed eaves with shaped corbels, arched entries and wood accents evoking traditional Spanish influences balance modern geometric forms, large windows, decks and balconies. Garages located at the rear leave front elevations unencumbered.

Inspired by Playa Vista's coastal location and climate, the architects made outdoor living central to the Trevion experience. Floorplans incorporate a large measure of flexibility in sync with modern lifestyles.

Modern Sensibilities

Central to the way these residences function is an open-concept floor plan, integrated outdoor living and thoughtful features, such as drop zones between garage and house, family-sized laundry rooms and ample storage. Plans offer four to five bedrooms and five-and-a-half baths. Well-proportioned master suites with a deck and beautifully appointed spa baths are positioned for privacy at one end of the second floor.

Multiple alternatives for some rooms allow Trevion to adapt to changing preferences. On the main level, a space designed as a bedroom is equally suitable for an office, kids' play area or media room. The second floor includes a lounge area, while a loft on the third floor offers unlimited potential from theater to gym to creative space.

Large windows and doors infuse interiors with daylight, but careful design maximizes privacy. Outdoor living is seamlessly integrated into multiple levels of the floorplan. A disappearing glass wall opens the great room and extends the main living outside. The elimination of any perceived change in elevation between the two spaces creates a flawless transition. This indoor-outdoor synergy energizes the entire plan.

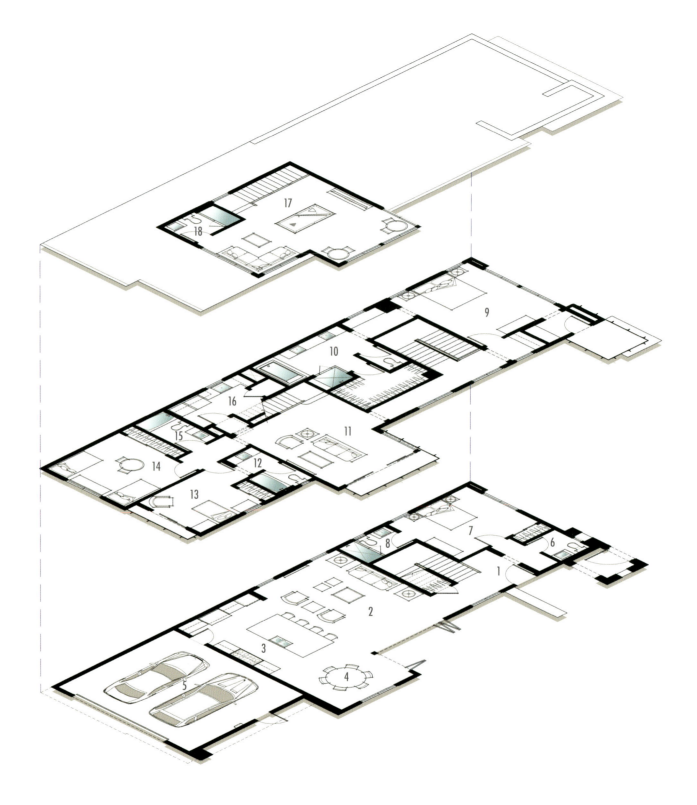

LEGEND

1. Entry
2. Great Room
3. Kitchen
4. Dining
5. Garage
6. Powder Room
7. Guest/Bedroom 4
8. Bath 4
9. Master Bedroom
10. Master Bath
11. Loft
12. Bath 2
13. Bedroom 2
14. Bedroom 3
15. Bath 3
16. Laundry
17. Bonus Room
18. Bath 5

3,453 SQUARE FEET
RESIDENCE ONE

About The Plan • There is no shortage of space in this home. Thoughtful positioning of rooms and outdoor living areas enhances the usable square footage. The plan unfolds in a logical sequence, centered around a kitchen-great room on the first level and a large lounge on the second. Bedrooms are situated for privacy with a generous allocation of space devoted to a master suite. Flexible spaces, such as the first-floor bedroom and third-level bonus room, enable owners to adapt the home to changing needs.

Above • With main living areas grouped around a side yard, the plan makes best use of a long narrow lot. Large retractable doors that wrap around the corner open the entire great room to outdoor spaces, which includes outdoor dining and seating in front of a fire.

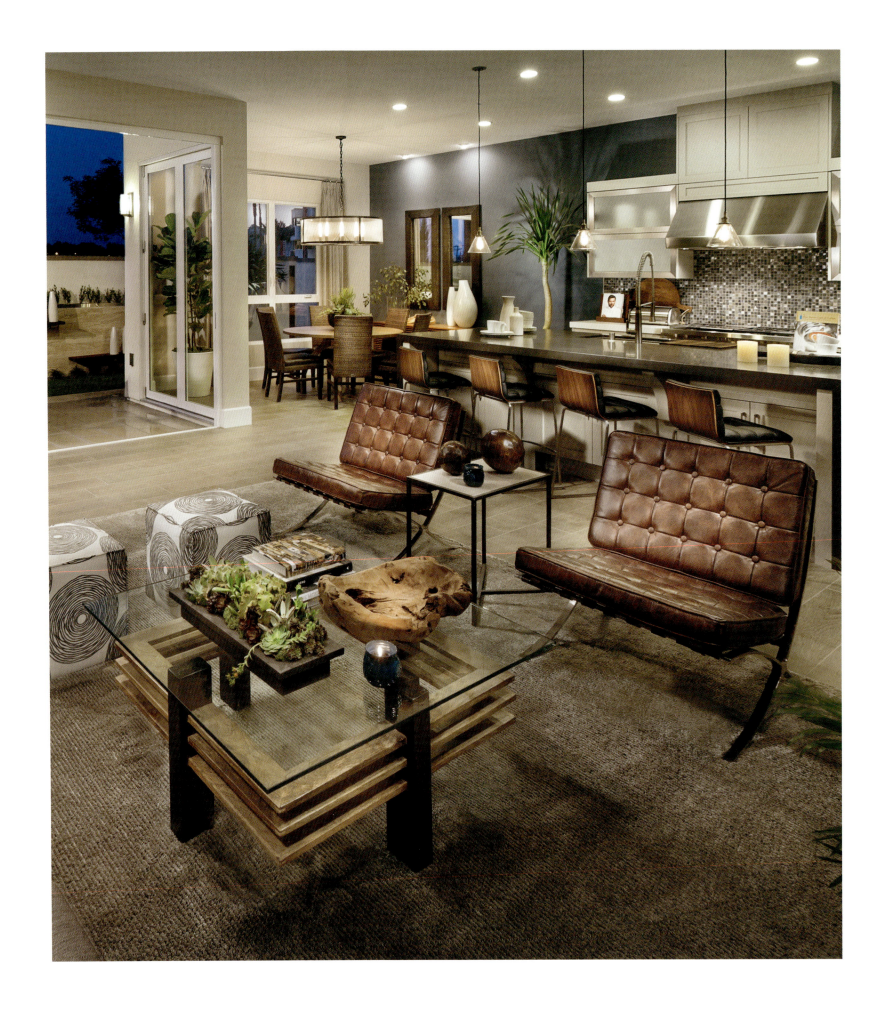

Left • Soft gray shaker cabinets add a transitional touch to great room and dining room, which are oriented toward the adjacent courtyard. Added pizzazz comes from a mosaic backsplash and glass-front cabinets.

Below • Eight-foot, wood-and-glass doors and stacked stone elevate the entry, pictured left. A large island, center, readies the kitchen for everything from afterschool cookies to cocktails. A location near the kitchen, right, makes al fresco dining easy.

Above • Stacking doors and flush threshold, center, merge the two main living areas, indoors and out. An entry courtyard, right, replaces an iconic front porch, creating an easy transition from street side to inside.

WOODSON

PLAYA VISTA, CALIFORNIA

Drawing inspiration from legendary architect Irving Gill, who defined LA's modern aesthetic, Woodson embraces this vernacular but tempers stark elevations with transitional elements.

Decks on the two top floors take advantage of views and coastal breezes, while a patio on the ground level continues the connection to the outdoors. Innovative interiors are eminently versatile with possibilities ranging from a master suite that occupies the entire third floor to a bedroom, home theater or creative space on the lower level — giving these homes a custom feel.

14

THE COMMUNITY

TRI POINTE HOMES, A MEMBER OF THE TRI POINTE GROUP

PACIFIC DIMENSIONS
APPLIED PHOTOGRAPHY

Top • Walls of glass incorporate extensive views as part of the interior. Exposed brick adds to a loft sensibility. A recessed niche for a TV on the media wall is one of many tech features.

Center • Corner windows work magic by opening up this office. The same treatment enhances a number of other rooms in Woodson.

Bottom • A patio adjacent to the game room and kitchen is an ideal venue for outdoor dining, relaxing or just catching the sunset.

Right • Transitional elements such as wood-siding accents, horizontal slat railings, warm stucco colors, and well-placed parapet walls show the new face of contemporary design in these exteriors.

Above • The room on the lower level, pictured left, is ideal for a game room or media center. Whimsical features such as this outdoor shower, right, make best use of found space and the surfboard shape echoes the coastal influence.

TRILOGY AT THE POLO CLUB
INDIO, CALIFORNIA

15

CLUBHOUSE
18,185 SQUARE FEET

SHEA HOMES

DESIGN LINES, INC.
A.G. PHOTOGRAPHY

The Polo Club, a clubhouse designed to foster connections among residents, becomes the virtual heart of this active lifestyle community in Indio. Further inspiration came from a desire to create a place that would nurture mind, body and spirit. Tapping into the duality of the desert, the design energizes while simultaneously promoting serenity and a sense of well-being.

On approach, the clubhouse, pictured above, appears to rise from the desert, offering a strong sense of place. A metal roof reinforces the overall contemporary aesthetic, while gables evoke the mountains that frame the setting. A massive stone wall bisects the structure and functions as an organizing axis with social spaces on one side and fitness and game areas on the other. It also directs attention through the building to the panorama on the other side and continues along extensive outdoor living areas, pictured right.

An Inspiring Oasis for Members

The club provides a valuable resource for members. In addition to a public restaurant, a casual gathering place for coffee and a full complement of fitness pursuits, the clubhouse also offers venues for private entertaining as well as wine lockers, game rooms and a showcase kitchen.

Like the clubhouse itself, the grand living room appears as an oasis — a place to refresh, energize and engage. Immense two-story glass walls visually connect the space with the desert setting and showcase the indoor-outdoor synergy central to the architecture. The rocky ridges of the Santa Rosa mountains form an undulating horizon in the distance, while trees and shrubs of the surrounding landscape provide a vibrant green backdrop. Adding to the impact and underscoring the overall design concept is the composition of rectangular shapes that comprise the glass wall.

Warm metals such as bronze window and door casings, as well as the earth tones of rustic stone, introduce transitional elements that balance the linear forms and soften the modern aesthetic. Yellow, which is the predominate hue throughout the building, injects even more warmth and energy. Artwork, liberal use of leather, light fixtures and accessories lend an equestrian feeling and connect the interior to the nearby polo club.

Above • A tensile structure and yellow canvas, similar to the nearby polo club, create a setting as dynamic as the views from this second-floor deck, a prime location for viewing dramatic desert sunsets. From here the panorama includes tennis and pickleball courts, a large event lawn and a lake that surrounds the rear of the building.

Below • The curves and arches of the resort pool, as well as the blue of the water, encourage an immediate relaxation response. The irregular shape creates many opportunities for poolside lounging. Once again, yellow is a vibrant accent. A 25-meter lap pool and a stand-alone fitness pool complete the pool area.

Water Everywhere

The club might be set in the middle of the Southern California desert, but water is integral to the experience. And, no matter where you are in the clubhouse, there is a good chance there will be a patch of blue in sight. A lake located on the backside of the building beyond the resort pools elevates the setting and the reflection of the clubhouse makes it seem almost magical.

NEW-CENTURY DESIGNS | 03

AXIS
RESIDENCE FOUR • WALL

AXIS
RESIDENCE THREE • FRAME

ELEMENTS OF DESIGN
FORMS + MASSING

AXIS
RESIDENCE ONE • SKY

EVERLY
THE COMMUNITY

MINIMALIST MODERN
PRIVATE RESIDENCE

91 SAN VICTOR
MULTI-FAMILY COMMUNITY

ELEMENTS OF DESIGN
COLORS + MATERIALS

ALTAIR
CLUBHOUSE

TOWN SQUARE
MASTER PLAN

AXIS

HENDERSON, NEVADA

16

RESIDENCE FOUR • WALL 4,470 SQUARE FEET

PARDEE HOMES, A MEMBER OF THE TRI POINTE GROUP

BOBBY BERK INTERIORS
A.G. PHOTOGRAPHY

This design is a game-changer, pushing transitional design to the borders of contemporary and beyond. The dynamic elevation, pictured above, makes a strong statement with a unique mix of forms, details and colors. Instant impressions are made with burnt-orange-hued stucco troweled to resemble plaster, a deep upper-level deck and a massive vertical stone wall that is a significant architectural and landscape element. The repetition of rectangular shapes throughout—from windows to entry doors and gates—brings harmony to dissimilar elements. The wall is an active feature bringing welcomed shade at different times of the day to several outdoor spaces, including the entry and interior courtyards. A soothing water feature and an angled courtyard ease the transition from the street.

About The Plan • The large stone wall, articulated on the elevation, bisects the structure and serves as the spine of the house, creating two separate wings bridged by the foyer and large shared courtyards. The main section of the house, formed on the left side of the wall, is comprised of the great room, kitchen and dining room. The section on the right includes a guest or multi-gen suite, as well as a family room and wine room. Stacking telescoping doors merge both sides with covered and open portions of the rear courtyard. On the second level, a large deck with a fireplace augments the master bedroom; secondary bedrooms also open to decks.

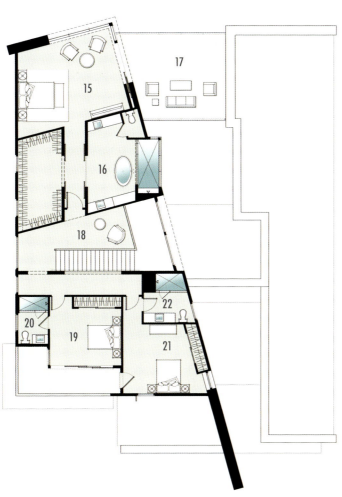

4,470 SQUARE FEET

LEGEND

1. Entry
2. Central Open Courtyard
3. Central Covered Courtyard
4. Den/Wine Room
5. Family
6. Laundry
7. Powder Room
8. Bath 4
9. Guest/Multi-Gen Suite
10. Powder Room
11. Kitchen
12. Dining
13. Great Room
14. Walk-in Pantry
15. Master Bedroom
16. Master Bath
17. Master Deck
18. Reading Loft
19. Bedroom 2
20. Bath 2
21. Bedroom 3
22. Bath 3
23. Covered Outdoor Family
24. Covered Outdoor Living
25. Garage

Luxury Refined

Left • Simple lines, beautifully executed, connote luxury today. The foyer, pictured top left, establishes this expectation for the entire house. A glass-enclosed wine storage and two-sided fireplace, bottom left, create engaging entertainment areas that expand onto a covered patio.

Above • The straightforward design of the master suite, pictured above, is enriched with natural materials. One portion of the room is a tranquil oasis, while large windows and telescoping doors open the other half to a private rooftop deck.

Mesmerizing Scene

Few outdoor living areas are as dynamic or exciting as this blend of covered and open spaces in the rear of Axis Wall. An outdoor kitchen, double-sided bar area and strategically lighted pathways promote an easy flow. A large covered lanai in the center merges both wings of the home. At the far end is the entry foyer, which opens to the front courtyard.

AXIS

HENDERSON, NEVADA

17

RESIDENCE THREE • FRAME 3,467 SQUARE FEET

PARDEE HOMES, A MEMBER OF THE TRI POINTE GROUP

YOLANDA LANDRUM INTERIOR DESIGN
A.G. PHOTOGRAPHY

In Axis Frame, the interplay of geometric shapes begins in the landscape and moves through all the elements that comprise the elevation, pictured above. Stone dominates with forms that are streamlined expressions of classic desert style. Windows and doors become striking accents, but the overall impression is calm and subdued. The sense of restraint continues inside, shown right, where an orderly progression of linear elements moves from foyer to great room to a showcase of technicolor sunsets and views of the Las Vegas strip. This home is oriented outwards, with impressive panoramas and an expansive array of outdoor spaces forming a backdrop for many of the rooms.

Above • Diversity and balance converge with great finesse in the great room, kitchen and entry. Recessed lighting calls attention to an unusual ceiling treatment in which soffits seem to float above the rooms, tying all three together. In the kitchen, a large soffit reinforces the shape of the island.

Above • Organic colors and natural materials make the otherwise contemporary spaces warm and inviting. A bar adjacent to the entry singles this out as a convivial house, designed for entertaining. A disappearing wall on the right extends the great room to a covered terrace.

Above • The kitchen is designed for ease and for serious cooking with glass-fronted cabinets that open upward and an oversized island. The geometric backsplash adds an additional textural element, while greenery, inside and out, injects a sense of vibrancy.

Right • Dark wood cabinets harmonize with elegant hues to showcase contemporary's new expression, which is warm and inviting. Wood grains further soften the overall impression.

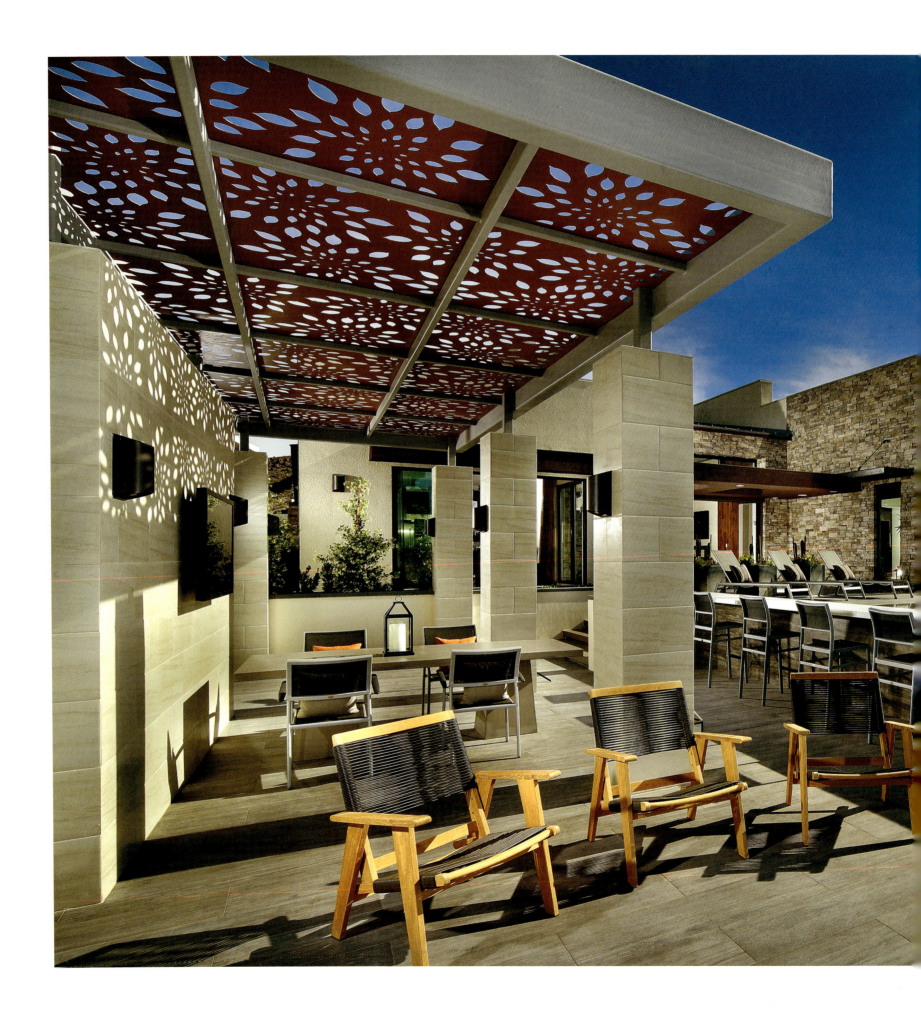

Waterscapes

A negative-edge pool with a swim-up bar enlivens the rear courtyard with as much kinetic energy as the views it takes in. A perforated design reminiscent of eyelet fabric makes an ever-changing light display over the covered outdoor dining. Stone- and wood-look tile on the patio and surrounding the pool lend a rustic, yet refined, ambiance to the entire scheme.

ELEMENTS OF DESIGN

FORMS + MASSING

Details often garner the most notice and attention in the design of a home. They are also a source to identify quality and information, but they are not the primary driver of a home's presence and pronunciation. Instead, it is form and mass that define architecture.

Mass is the sense of the weight, while form interprets and gives expression. Traditional design, which in the United States has mostly Euro-centric roots, employs basic form and mass.

Transitional design takes the recognizable interplay between form and mass and begins to reinterpret it in simpler methods. Generally, it is safe to assume that transitional architecture lightens massing by simplifying components of the structure. For example, instead of predictable symmetric shapes and placement, glazing in transitional design opens walls and sometimes corners.

Advancements in technology facilitate this process with new products that allow large and unobstructed openings in the mass. Therefore, expansive use of doors and windows becomes a transitional signature and is central to the design of every home featured in this book.

In the continuum, as transitional moves closer to contemporary, traditional references diminish and are replaced by cleaner abstracted compositions. This movement dictates scrutiny, as even the smallest aspect of the structure must seem essential, purposeful and well-studied rather than applied or decorative. Success in the execution of this simplified, yet new, vocabulary in form and massing deserves the designer's full attention.

AXIS

HENDERSON, NEVADA

18

RESIDENCE ONE • SKY   3,762 SQUARE FEET

PARDEE HOMES, A MEMBER OF THE TRI POINTE GROUP

YOLANDA LANDRUM INTERIOR DESIGN
A.G. PHOTOGRAPHY

Transitional design may glance back, but is always looking forward. Axis Sky takes materials and forms characteristic of desert architecture to the next level with a fresh new interpretation. No longer an amenity, outdoor living becomes central to function and lifestyle. Stone grounds the elevation, pictured above, with a sense of implied mass, while pale hues lighten the overall impression, as do low-slung roof lines and deep overhangs. The focus in Sky is a vibrant interior courtyard. Angles in the elevation direct attention toward the entry and sightlines extend inward. A water feature previews the sense of refreshment and respite from the desert sun found inside. The exterior stone continues into an impressive foyer, pictured right, further anchoring the home with a visual tie between inside and out.

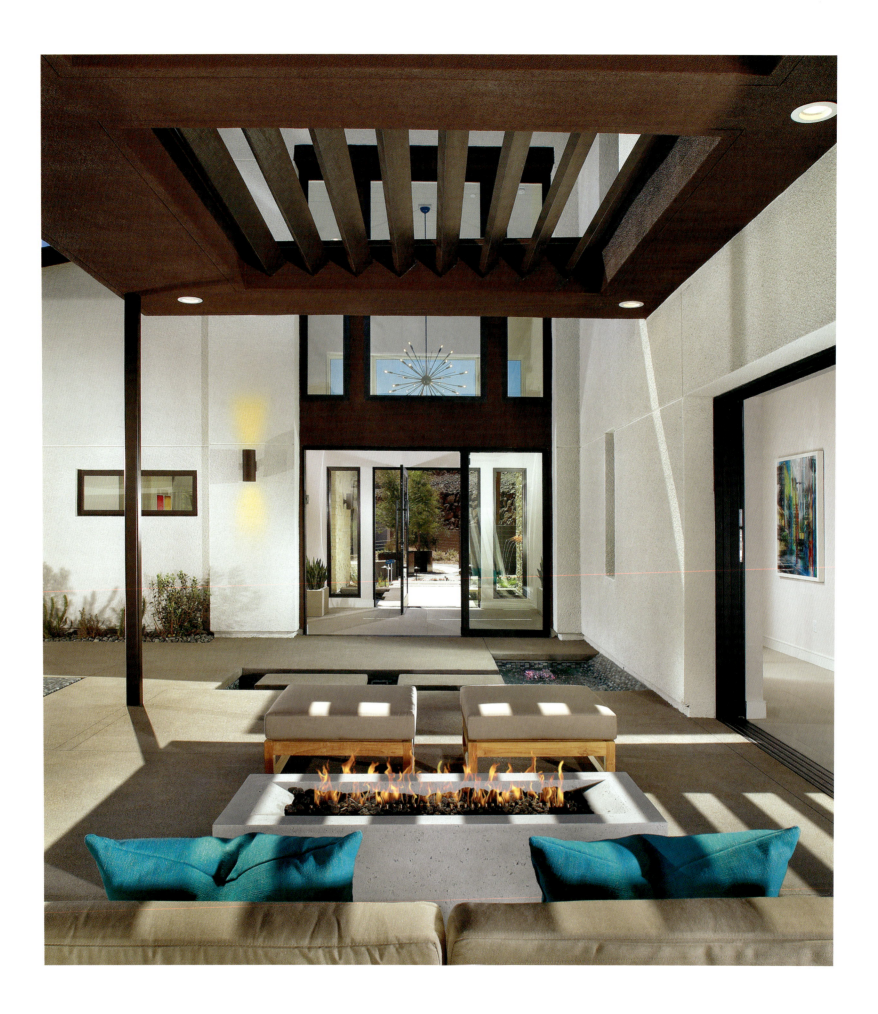

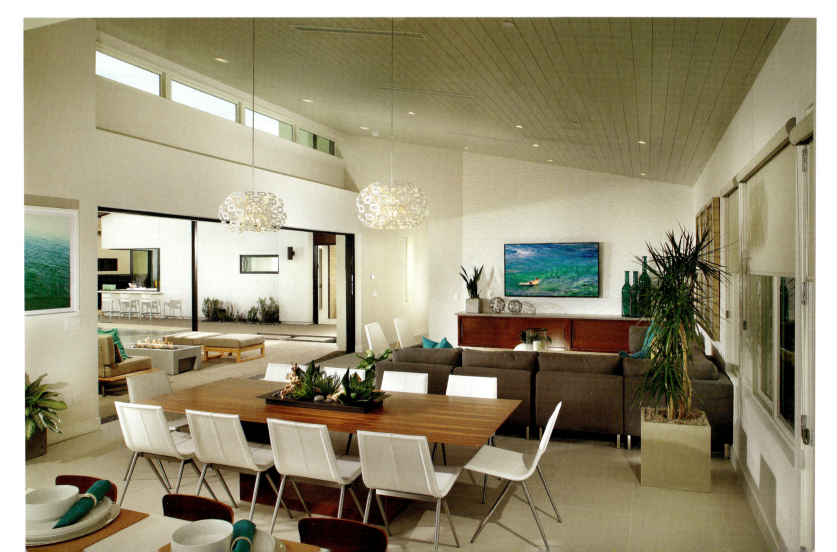

Above • A lowered ceiling carves out the kitchen as a separate space. Windows along one wall introduce another dimension, more natural light and hillside vistas.

Left • Major rooms including the master bedroom, pictured top left, are arranged around the interior courtyard. Sunlight and views via a narrow window enhance bathing in the generous master bath, lower left.

Top • The interior courtyard is composed of a mix of outdoor spaces. The perspective from the right corner of the spa highlights the progression from great room to covered lanai to open air.

Center • Outfitted with a bar and oriented to capture views of rolling hilltops, this lounge area, unlike the rest of the house, directs attention outward. A pergola over the deck moderates the impact of the intense desert sun.

Bottom • Angles converge to embrace the interior courtyard in this revealing drone shot, which also illustrates how important outdoor living is to the home. The foyer and entry pavilion, centered on the left side of the photo, lead directly outside to a covered terrace next to the great room.

About The Plan • This plan is designed to wrap around an internal courtyard with a pool and multiple outdoor living areas. Located on the first floor, the kitchen/great room/dining areas all expand into the internal courtyard, as does the private master bedroom suite.

Unique are the two guest wings apart from the main living areas—one, a contained space on the first floor to the right of the entry, and the other a second-floor space with a lounge area, separate bedroom and bath. Both areas offer tremendous flexibility that allows each owner to create the right living environment.

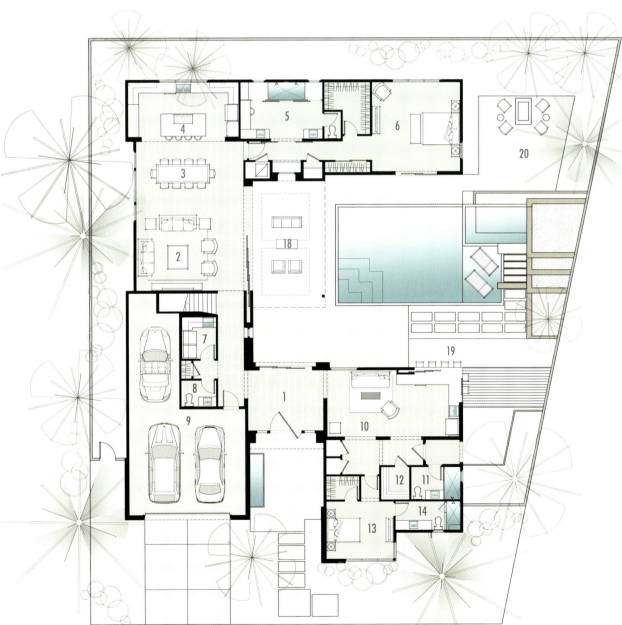

LEGEND

1. Entry
2. Great Room
3. Dining
4. Kitchen
5. Master Bath
6. Master Bedroom
7. Laundry
8. Powder Room
9. Garage
10. Flex/Multi-Gen Suite
11. Pool Bath/Bath 3
12. Sauna
13. Guest Bedroom
14. Guest Bath/Bath 4
15. Bedroom 2
16. Bath 2
17. Loft/Lounge Area
18. Covered Terrace
19. Pool Bar
20. Outdoor Retreat

3,762 SQUARE FEET

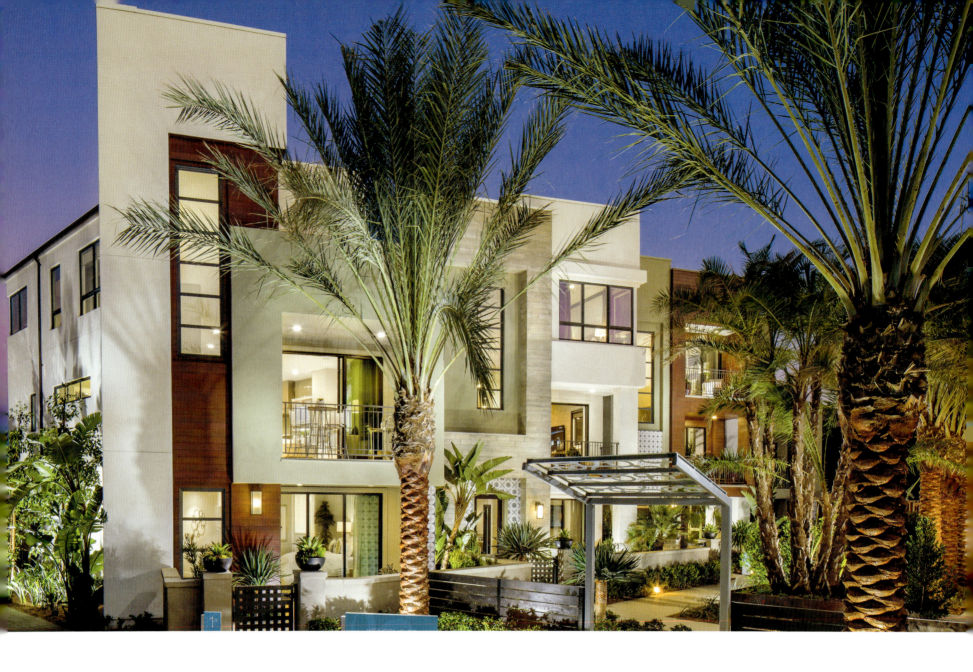

EVERLY

PLAYA VISTA, CALIFORNIA

Taken literally, the word contemporary means "of today," and no other phrase better describes Everly. In this iteration of the modern vernacular, an interplay of geometric forms, showcased by stone and stucco, makes a strong statement. Windows, decks and doors become architectural elements. The overall impact is one of consistency, even though each home bears a distinct identity. The end result is an elevation that is at once streamlined and detailed, calming yet dynamic.

19

THE COMMUNITY

BROOKFIELD RESIDENTIAL

CDC DESIGNS
ERIC FIGGE PHOTOGRAPHY

Top • Decks and patios extend the living outdoors, while expanses of windows open the interior in this great room. Steps lead to a dramatic light-filled stairwell and the third floor.

Center • This kitchen becomes a hub for all the main-floor activities. A walk-in pantry is nearby. The hallway leads to a full bath and adaptable space.

Bottom • Used as an office, this room on the main floor yields options ranging from a hideaway for guests to music room, media center or play area.

Left • The elevation is a symphony of shapes and materials.

Right • Concrete tile wrapped around the rectangular form turns a column of windows into an artful element. Underneath, a tile surround with a geometric motif elevates the entry. Windows and doors add to the layering of linear shapes.

Above • This generous kitchen energizes all the surrounding spaces. The mix of cabinets, use of light and upscale ambiance are desired features today. A slight angle produced by the home's boomerang footprint sets the great room apart without disrupting the spatial flow.

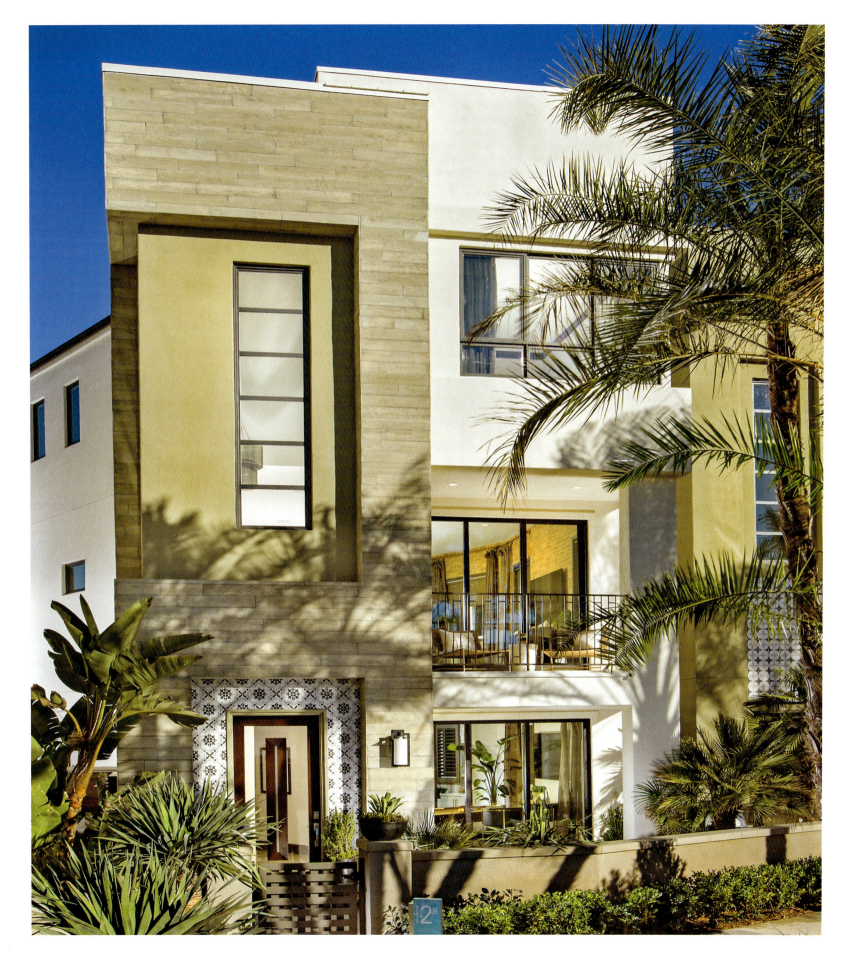

MINIMALIST MODERN

LOS ANGELES COUNTY, CALIFORNIA

Something contemporary and cool was the owners' request for this private residence, and the end result is considered a little gem in the neighborhood. The architecture draws inspiration from the Bauhaus movement. The forms reference the clean lines of contemporary with a fresh new expression that is approachable. Stucco is used throughout, but changes in color and texture add interest to the elevation, pictured above, while highlighting the overall linear composition and calling attention to the forms and massing.

20

PRIVATE RESIDENCE • 2,872 SQUARE FEET

A.G. PHOTOGRAPHY

Left • Patterns in the large windows over the garage, as well as the tall windows in the corner, echo the geometric conversation in the elevation, while also infusing interiors with light.

Top Right • Dark treads and risers, energized by the kinetic sense of the black balustrades, turn the stairway into an artful focal point. A wine cellar makes best use of space under the stairway; the horizontal configuration of the racking becomes another element in the geometric interplay.

Bottom Right • The juxtaposition of dark and light continues in the kitchen, where contrasting elements such as the cabinets and a long island highlight the linear features of the interior.

About The Plan • Meticulous attention to detail makes best use of every square foot from wine storage tucked under the stairs to the walk-in pantry. The plan ensures a place for everyone, including a first-floor guest suite and a teen loft on the upper level. Strategic placement of windows in the front and rear lends a sense of openness to the home, which is located on a long narrow lot.

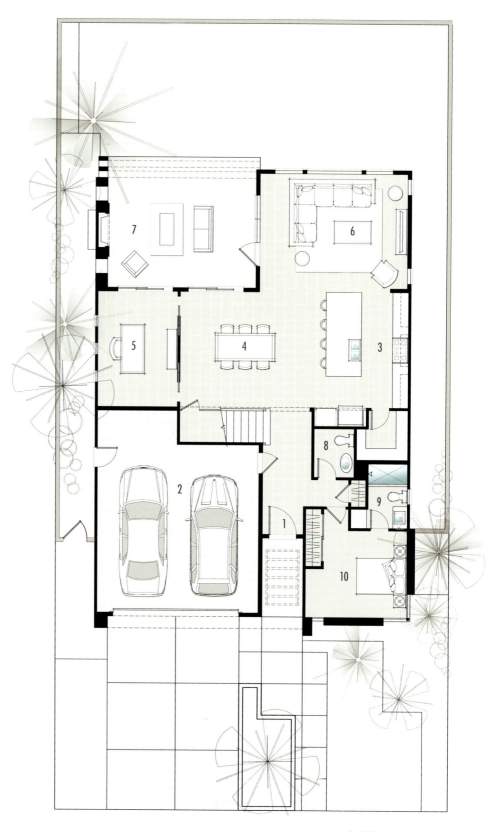

LEGEND

1. Entry
2. Garage
3. Kitchen
4. Dining
5. Home Office/Library
6. Great Room
7. California Room
8. Powder Room
9. Guest Bath/Bath 4
10. Guest/Bedroom 4
11. Master Bedroom
12. Master Bath
13. Bedroom 2
14. Bedroom 3
15. Bath 3
16. Teen Loft
17. Laundry

Right • A California room with a fireplace and television, pictured above, energizes kitchen, great room and office. Geometric cutouts on the facing wall enhance the open feeling with vignettes of the landscape without compromising privacy. Forms and mass define the rear elevation, pictured below.

2,872 SQUARE FEET

21
MULTI-FAMILY COMMUNITY

91 SAN VICTOR
SCOTTSDALE, ARIZONA

CALATLANTIC HOMES

PACIFIC DIMENSIONS, INC.
A.G. PHOTOGRAPHY

This gated community in central Scottsdale offers a unique interpretation of the duplex concept with two stacked flats, rather than side-by-side homes, in each building. Architecturally, the plan pushes the boundaries of transitional design with few, if any, historical references. Instead, it is purely modern in form and appears in the elevation, pictured far right, as an expressive composition of blocks accentuated with punches of color and varied textures. On both the inside and outside, the pattern of the windows, as well as corner and floor-to-ceiling placements, enhance the contemporary sensibility.

A strong connection to greenspace is integral to the design. Covered decks and patios, positioned for privacy, extend living spaces on both levels. A stucco wall encloses patios and augments the square footage of ground-level units.

Left • Each building is just under 60-feet wide, creating single-floor residences that range from 1,361 square feet to 2,159 square feet. Upper-level homes offer an expansive open-concept space, pictured top left, with a study or office adjacent to the main living area. Garages are located along a rear alleyway, shown bottom right.

Below • Buildings are arranged around a central greenspace. When viewed together, the colors, patterns and rhythm of the varied elevations make a distinctive architectural statement. In addition to community open space, outdoor amenities include a pool, covered ramada with a kitchen and a fire pit.

Left • The style and placement of windows are contemporary elements in the elevation. An overlay of materials and robust colors enhance the design by adding a sense of mass and directing attention to structural elements. The end result is a lively, exciting composition.

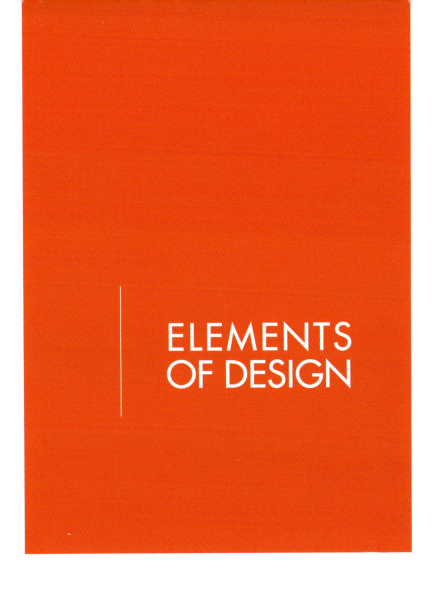

ELEMENTS OF DESIGN

COLORS + MATERIALS

Transitional architecture draws from the essence of established styles such as Spanish, Mediterranean and even Mid-Century Modern, blending familiar details with fresh shapes and forms to create an original vocabulary. This amalgamation of old and new creates a new language of colors and materials designed to highlight linear components and unique silhouettes without disrupting their elegant simplicity. Materials themselves might be considered transitional and, though tied to honored sources, help blaze an entirely new path.

Materials used for transitional designs reflect traditional construction and might appear to be derived from nature, but increasingly they result from innovative manufacturing processes. Inventive cement tiles can be finished in a variety of ways, including replicating Moorish designs. Advanced composites and engineered products are often used in cladding to emulate wood, iron or other metals. A good example is the façade of the Contemporary Transitional, shown on the facing page top left, where an engineered material mimics Corten steel.

Stone adds texture, creates focal points and, in instances such as the Wall residence, shown on the facing page top right, strengthens an essential element and helps define the architecture. What often facilitates these applications is the use of a manufactured stone that so closely resembles the real thing, only those with a trained eye can tell the difference. Like other new materials, it is less expensive, easy to insulate, available in a range of profiles and allows for novel applications, giving designers more control over size, color and profile.

Stucco is another traditional material widely utilized in transitional designs, but new techniques create a variety of appearances. A steel-trowel finish that incorporates lime has a softer sensibility and is ideal for deep saturated pigments. Another applied-stucco finish replicates the color and texture of concrete.

Regarding color, this new form of architecture calls for outside-the-box thinking. Unlike white, black, brown and gray favored by traditional design, transitional embraces intense hues in unconventional combinations. For many of the desert settings in this book, designers have keyed into richer colors and more jewel tones. Rather than simply a highlight application for trim, colors call out transitional forms and shapes, highlighting their role in the overall elevation. Materials and colors are often treated as separate entities; however, transitional combines both elements in carefully controlled harmony.

22 | ALTAIR

CLUBHOUSE • 11,792 SQUARE FEET

HERITAGE HILLS, IRVINE, LLC

IRVINE, CALIFORNIA

Old stone lends a historic sense to an entirely modern clubhouse intended for residents of the 11 neighborhoods that comprise this new upscale community. Two walls, clad with stone, bisect the building and serve as points of organization for this multi-purpose structure. The mass of the stone emphasizes the grounding of the overall structure. The curving lines of the outside edge of the pool are a perfect contrast to the overall linear scheme. Similar to a sports club, this building houses a gym, lounge with seating, a coffee bar, restaurant and many multi-purpose rooms, each of which has adjacent covered outdoor areas. At the far end, interior spaces lead to a large event lawn. Along the pool, raised beds in zig-zag patterns call attention to surrounding trees and balance the line of cabanas.

TOWN SQUARE

DUBAI, UNITED ARAB EMIRATES

23

MODERN TOWN CENTER • MASTER PLAN

NSHAMA

LIFANG ASSOCIATES
MATSMA CONSULTING & DEVELOPMENT
MICHAEL ABBOTT ASSOCIATES
SQUINT OPERA

Little more than a half-hour from downtown Dubai, a new community is redefining the concept of a town center. Town Square has established a new paradigm for large-scale master planning and mixed-use development. As in other major cities, years of skyrocketing prices in Dubai effectively closed the housing market to middle-income earners. The concept behind Town Square Dubai is a response to this need, and the focus on mid-market makes it unprecedented, as does the emphasis on social engagement. When the build-out is complete, there will be a projected 85,000 residents living in a mix of townhomes and high-rise buildings, enjoying retail and parks spread across 882 acres. Greenspaces and sheltering gardens abound, as do paths for the outdoor experience.

Multiple venues and opportunities to foster connections are integral to the plan. A vibrant town center and urban park is a short walk from residences. This half-mile-long greenspace is lined with shops, restaurants and cafes, as well as a high-end hotel. Comparable in size to St. Mark's Square, the park incorporates water features, sport courts, recreation areas geared to every age group, meditative gardens, jogging paths, skate parks, a giant screen for outdoor films, and even a carousel.

What really sets Town Square apart is the scale of the project, not just geographically, but also in terms of the number of residences. Devising a plan to meet these requirements, while also taking into account climate restrictions, psychosocial needs and the fundamentals of day-to-day life, entailed extensive research worldwide, along with the acumen to take that knowledge to the next level. The plan above shows the distribution of residential buildings and greenspace and the connectivity of the central core, which is designated by the large central rectangle. High-rises at the corner anchor this park; adjacent squares include buildings ranging from ten to twenty stories. Two-story townhouses, clustered in a number of squares throughout, are surrounded by trees in neighborhoods that include a park or pockets of greenspace as well as pools. Schools and a stadium are located at the far end of the plan. Early visions called for more mid-rise buildings, but as the design progressed more high-rises were included, and these vertical structures act as much-needed points of orientation for such a large area.

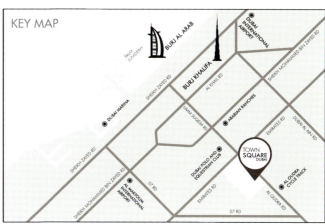

This map of Dubai, right, shows the proximity of Town Square to Burj Khalifa, the tallest building in the world.

Above • Wide sidewalks and paths, coupled with activities for a range of ages, invite participation in the central square and park. Town Square includes 600 retail outlets, a twelve-kilometer network of trails and 154,000 square meters of parks.

Future Sensibilities

Behind every aspect of Town Square is a consideration of how adaptable it will be for the future. This is particularly true for residential buildings. Plans for individual residences maximize square footage and include a mix of one, two and three bedrooms as well as two-story penthouses. Balconies incorporate an indoor/outdoor synergy which is enhanced with extensive use of glass.

In the buildings, pictured right, residents are only an elevator ride away from all the vibrancy of the community. The first two levels are devoted to commercial use, while the third level is an amenity space that includes a pool, gardens, play area, even a place to run. Strong horizontal shapes add to the contemporary nature of the exterior.

Throughout Town Square, great attention was paid to the landscape. Boulevards and walkways are typically shaded by a canopy of trees, and the community is bounded by a green area. Greenspaces also define neighborhoods. Some might call this development an oasis in the desert, but for those who live here it is simply home.

PROJECT SUMMARY

ANNOTATED PROJECTS LIST

01 MODERN FARMHOUSE
RESIDENCE
HENDERSON, NEVADA

Builder: Pardee Homes, a member of the TRI Pointe Group

Landscape Architect: AndersonBaron
Interior Designer: Bobby Berk Interiors + Design
Structural Engineer: BORM International

Photographer: Chris Mayer Photography

Awards:
Gold Nugget Awards
The Nationals

02 CONTEMPORARY TRANSITIONAL
RESIDENCE
HENDERSON, NEVADA

Builder: Pardee Homes, a member of the TRI Pointe Group

Landscape Architect: AndersonBaron
Interior Designer: Bobby Berk Interiors + Design
Structural Engineer: BORM International

Photographer: Chris Mayer Photography

03 ESCALA
RESIDENCE TWO
HENDERSON, NEVADA

Builder: Pardee Homes, a member of the TRI Pointe Group

Landscape Architect: AndersonBaron
Interior Designer: Bobby Berk Interiors + Design
Structural Engineer: BORM International

Photographer: Chris Mayer Photography

Awards:
Gold Nugget Awards
The Nationals

04 VERMILLION
THE COMMUNITY
PALM SPRINGS, CALIFORNIA

Builder: Beazer Homes

Landscape Architect: David Neault Associates
Interior Designer: Triomphe Design
Structural Engineer: Option-One Consulting Engineers

Photographer: A.G. Photography

Awards:
Best in American Living Awards

05 TRILOGY AT VISTANCIA
THE COMMUNITY
PEORIA, ARIZONA

Builder: Shea Homes

Landscape Architect: BlueStar
Interior Designer: Design Lines Inc.
Structural Engineer: Felten Group

Photographer: Mark Boisclair Photography

Awards:
Best in American Living Awards
Gold Nugget Awards
The Nationals

06 PRAIRE-INSPIRED CONTEMPORARY
PRIVATE RESIDENCE
LOS GATOS, CALIFORNIA

Builder: Davidon Homes

Landscape Architect: Ken Schoppet
Interior Designer: Tate Lee Design
Structural Engineer: Gouvis Engineering

Photographer: Chris Mayer Photography

07 BEACH RESIDENCE
PRIVATE RESIDENCE
CAYUCOS, CALIFORNIA

Builder: Owner and Nordic Builders

Landscape Architect: Owner
Interior Designer: Interior Specialists, Inc.
Structural Engineer: Gouvis Engineering

Photographer: Chris Mayer Photography

Awards:
Gold Nugget Awards

08 LEGACY CLUB AT GREENWOOD
COMMUNITY BUILDING
TUSTIN, CALIFORNIA

Builder: Standard Pacific Homes

Landscape Architect: Valleycrest Design Group
Interior Designer: Ver Designs
Structural Engineer: Dale Christian Structural Engineer

Photographer: A.G. Photography

Awards:
The Nationals

09 ARTESANA
RESIDENCE ONE
SAN DIEGO, CALIFORNIA

Builder: Pardee Homes, a member of the TRI Pointe Group

Landscape Architect: C2 Collaborative
Interior Designer: Ami Samuels Interiors
Structural Engineer: Gouvis Engineering
Photographer: Eric Figge Photography

Awards:
Gold Nugget Awards

10 ARTESANA
RESIDENCE TWO
SAN DIEGO, CALIFORNIA

Builder: Pardee Homes, a member of the TRI Pointe Group

Landscape Architect: C2 Collaborative
Interior Designer: Ami Samuels Interiors
Structural Engineer: Gouvis Engineering
Photographer: Eric Figge Photography

Awards:
Gold Nugget Awards

11 ARTESANA
RESIDENCE THREE
SAN DIEGO, CALIFORNIA

Builder: Pardee Homes, a member of the TRI Pointe Group

Landscape Architect: C2 Collaborative
Interior Designer: Ami Samuels Interiors
Structural Engineer: Gouvis Engineering
Photographer: Eric Figge Photography

Awards:
Gold Nugget Awards

12 CASAVIA
THE COMMUNITY
SAN DIEGO, CALIFORNIA

Builder: Pardee Homes, a member of the TRI Pointe Group

Landscape Architect: LandCreativeInc.
Interior Designer: Studio V Interior Design
Structural Engineer: Gouvis Engineering

Photographer: Chris Mayer Photography

Awards:
Gold Nugget Awards
The Nationals

13 TREVION
THE COMMUNITY
PLAYA VISTA, CALIFORNIA

Builder: Brookfield Residential

Landscape Architect: C2 Collaborative
Interior Designer: Yolanda Landrum Interior Design
Structural Engineer: BORM International

Photographer: Aron Photography

Awards:
Best in American Living Awards
Gold Nugget Awards
The Nationals

14 WOODSON
THE COMMUNITY
PLAYA VISTA, CALIFORNIA

Builder: Pardee Homes, a member of the TRI Pointe Group

Landscape Architect: C2 Collaborative
Interior Designer: Pacific Dimensions Inc.
Structural Engineer: VCA Structural

Photographer: Applied Photography

Awards:
Best in American Living Awards
Gold Nugget Awards

15 TRILOGY
AT THE POLO CLUB
CLUBHOUSE
INDIO, CALIFORNIA

Builder: Shea Homes

Landscape Architect: iN2iT Studio
Interior Designer: Design Lines, Inc.
Structural Engineer: Dale Christian Structural Engineer

Photographer: A.G. Photography

16 AXIS
RESIDENCE FOUR • WALL
HENDERSON, NEVADA

Builder: Pardee Homes, a member of the TRI Pointe Group

Landscape Architect: AndersonBaron
Interior Designer: Bobby Berk Interiors + Design
Structural Engineer: BORM International

Photographer: A.G. Photography

Awards:
Gold Nugget Awards

17 AXIS
RESIDENCE THREE • FRAME
HENDERSON, NEVADA

Builder: Pardee Homes, a member of the TRI Pointe Group

Landscape Architect: AndersonBaron
Interior Designer: Yolanda Landrum Interior Design
Structural Engineer: BORM International

Photographer: A.G. Photography

Awards:
Gold Nugget Awards

18 AXIS
RESIDENCE ONE • SKY
HENDERSON, NEVADA

Builder: Pardee Homes, a member of the TRI Pointe Group

Landscape Architect: AndersonBaron
Interior Designer: Yolanda Landrum Interior Design
Structural Engineer: BORM International

Photographer: A.G. Photography

Awards:
Gold Nugget Awards

19 EVERLY
THE COMMUNITY
PLAYA VISTA, CALIFORNIA

Builder: Brookfield Residential

Landscape Architect: C2 Collaborative
Interior Designer: CDC Designs
Structural Engineer: VCA Structural

Photographer: Eric Figge Photography

Awards:
Best in American Living Awards
Gold Nugget Awards
The Nationals

20 MINIMALIST MODERN
PRIVATE RESIDENCE
LOS ANGELES COUNTY, CALIFORNIA

Interior Designer: Owner
Structural Engineer: Option-One Consulting Engineers

Photographer: A.G. Photography

21 91 SAN VICTOR
MULTI-FAMILY COMMUNITY
SCOTTSDALE, ARIZONA

Builder: CalAtlantic Homes

Landscape Architect: LVA Design Studio
Interior Designer: Pacific Dimensions Inc.
Structural Engineer: Felten Group

Photographer: A.G. Photography

22 ALTAIR
CLUBHOUSE
IRVINE, CALIFORNIA

Builder: Heritage Hills Irvine, LLC
Landscape Architect: C2 Collaborative

23 TOWN SQUARE
MASTER PLAN
DUBAI, UNITED ARAB EMIRATES

Builder: Nshama

Renderers:
Lifang Associates
Matsma Consulting & Development
Michael Abbott & Associates
Squint/Opera

Awards:
Gold Nugget Awards

STAFF

EXECUTIVES
Aram Bassenian
Carl Lagoni
Jeff LaFetra
David Kosco
Scott Adams
Hans Anderle
Robert Chavez
Steven Dewan
Jeff Ganyo
Mark Kiner
Brian Neves
Ken Niemerski
Lee Rogaliner
Cindy Teale

DIRECTOR OF MARKETING
Heather McCune

SENIOR VICE PRESIDENTS
Marty Lopez
Gary Penman

SENIOR VICE PRESIDENT, CHINA OPERATIONS
Yao Wang

VICE PRESIDENTS
George Handy
Edie Motoyama

SENIOR ASSOCIATES
Sophia Braverman
Arnel Casanova
Jeff Marcotte
Milo Olea
Tony Vinh

ASSOCIATES
Daniel Lee
Phillip Lee
Zsombor Nagy
Alan Nguyen
Teressa Oehrlein
Ashutosh Pant
Jeff Roach
Michael Stone

STAFF
Kirk Adams
Lizeth Benitez
Anthony Bennett
Brian Cameron
Felipe Chaidez
Susan Chan
Luis Chavez
Johnny Chung
Rachel Crichton
Ryan Decker
Sue Dewan
Matthew Esqueda
Mark Felicetta
Jornell Franciliso
Jina Freeman
Vannessa Fusi-Hoblit
Montserrat Gilmore
Bradley Green
Brenda Gutierrez
Zafar Hadi
Heather Handing
Young Hong
Gregg Johnson
Si Kim
Brian Li
Jeff Lin
Ed Lopez
Cortney McGerty
Carlos Meneses
Aaron Mick
Christina Miramontes
Kim Mohr
Eileah Monson
Gina Najm
Rafael Navarro
Abigail Ng
Thang Ngo
Jackie Tran
Louisa Nip
Ronnie Ojeda
Ray Olaes
Carlos Olivares
Juan Olvera
Daniel Oyakawa
Mia Patterson
Duff Paulsen
Susan Pistacchi
Herman Poon
Vandad Rohbani
Ryan Rosecrans
Sarah Sha
Abegail Sumarinas
Princess Ta
Eric Tigno
Trey Tillman
Chris Velasquez
Shane Viernes
April Villa
Garrett Wilkinson
Yuying Yeh
Kyle Zaleski